MY FIRST PONY

Danny Pate

Michael Beas

ISBN: 978-1-962825-06-1

TABLE OF CONTENTS

FOREWORD

GREETINGS, FELLOW HORSE ENTHUSIASTS, AND YOUNG riders. It is with immense pleasure and a deep sense of nostalgia that I write this foreword for the enchanting book, *My First Pony*. As the founder of Atlas Elite Publishing and co-founder of Beas Family Farms alongside my incredible wife, Kristine Kennedy-Beas, I have had the privilege of witnessing the transformative power that horses hold in the lives of individuals, especially during those precious moments spent with their first pony.

My First Pony takes us on a delightful journey, back to the days when our inner passion for horses began to grow. With each turn of the page, we are transported to a time when the world was filled with wonder, and our hearts were ignited by the presence of these majestic creatures. The stories woven within this book capture the essence of the unique bond between a child and their first pony; a bond that forever shapes their character and sets them on a path of lifelong devotion to these remarkable animals.

Throughout my own journey with horses, I have witnessed firsthand the extraordinary impact that these gentle beings have on our lives. They teach us invaluable lessons about responsibility, patience, and the power of connection. From the moment we lay eyes on our first pony, a connection is forged that goes beyond words. It is a silent understanding, a partnership built on trust, and a friendship that withstands the test of time.

In *My First Pony*, the author skillfully brings to life the memories and emotions associated with this pivotal moment in a young rider's life. The vivid descriptions and heartfelt anecdotes resonate with horse lovers of all ages, sparking fond recollections of our own cherished equine companions. We are reminded of the joyous adventures, the shared laughter, and the unforgettable milestones that make the bond between a child and their first pony so indelible.

As co-founder of Beas Family Farms, I have had the honor of witnessing the transformative journey of countless individuals as they discover the magic of horses. From our sprawling pastures to the serene stables, our farm serves as a haven where both horse and human find solace, understanding, and unconditional love. It is within these hallowed grounds that the seeds of equestrian dreams are sown and nurtured, laying the foundation for a lifelong passion.

To the young readers embarking on their own equestrian odyssey, I offer my heartfelt congratulations and a gentle word of encouragement. Cherish the moments spent with your first pony, for they hold within them the power to shape your future and ignite a lifelong dedication to these magnificent creatures. Allow yourself to be captivated by the magic of the horse, and let their wisdom guide you on your journey towards becoming an accomplished equestrian.

I extend my deepest gratitude to the author of *My First Pony* for capturing the essence of this extraordinary bond in such a captivating manner. Through their words, they have bestowed upon us a timeless treasure that celebrates the profound impact of our first pony and reminds us of the joys that await those who embark on this remarkable journey.

Dear readers, I invite you to immerse yourselves in the pages of *My First Pony* and relish in the stories that unfold. Allow yourselves to be transported to a time of innocence, wonder, and the unbreakable bond between a child and their first pony. May this book reignite your love for these extraordinary creatures and serve as a source of inspiration for generations of equestrians to come.

Wishing you all an enchanting reading experience and a lifelong appreciation for the extraordinary magic that horses bring into our lives.

ACKNOWLEDGMENTS

I WOULD LIKE TO EXTEND MY HEARTFELT GRATITUDE TO THE individuals who have played pivotal roles in shaping my journey as an author. Their support, encouragement, and unwavering belief in my passion have been instrumental in bringing this book to fruition.

First and foremost, I am immensely grateful to Shawn and Natalie Russell for their generous hospitality and for welcoming me into their home. Their introduction to several experienced riders in the equestrian world provided invaluable insights that have found their way into the pages of this book.

I owe a special debt of thanks to Don and Nancy Stewart for their invaluable guidance and for introducing me to the world of athletes. Their mentorship has been invaluable in enriching the narrative and adding depth to the characters within.

A heartfelt appreciation goes to Rolf and Jennifer Bauersachs for their introduction to the esteemed Wellington Group. Their connections have opened doors and provided me with invaluable perspectives, adding authenticity to the story's backdrop.

To my sister Madge Caldwell, my brother Jack, and his wife Teressa Pate, I am deeply grateful for their unwavering support and patience throughout the decade-long journey of crafting this book. Their willingness to listen to my wild ideas and put up with me during the writing process has been a constant source of motivation.

Additionally, I would like to express my thanks to Michael Beas and Kristine Kennedy Beas for their encouragement and support during the publishing process and for helping make this dream a reality.

To everyone who has been a part of this journey, whether directly or indirectly, your influence has left an indelible mark on this work. Your belief in my abilities has been a driving force, and I am sincerely grateful for each one of you.

With heartfelt appreciation,

Danny Pate

I AM PROFOUNDLY GRATEFUL TO THE EXCEPTIONAL INDIVIDU-
als who played pivotal roles in bringing this book to fruition. Foremost, my heartfelt thanks go to my wife, Kristine
Kennedy Beas, whose influence brought me closer to my
passion for horses. To my two sons, Michael Lazaro Beas and
Alex Noah Beas, and my daughter, Schamy Nieme, your unwavering support, love, and understanding have been my constant inspiration.

Kristine, your enduring patience, encouragement, and belief in
me have been the driving force behind this endeavor. Your love
serves as the anchor that grounds me, and I am profoundly grateful for your presence in my life.

I extend my appreciation to my dedicated team, Dar Dowling
and Tom Colleran, whose professionalism and commitment
were invaluable throughout this journey. Your collaboration and
tireless efforts elevated this project to new heights, and I am
genuinely fortunate to have such a talented and devoted team.

A heartfelt thank you is extended to my dear friend Danny Pate,
whose passion for horses has not only inspired me but also
served as a guiding light. Your genuine love for these majestic
creatures has imparted to me the true meaning of dedication and
enthusiasm.

To everyone who has been part of this journey, thank you for
your unwavering support, encouragement, and belief in the vi-
sion of this book. Your contributions have left an indelible mark,
and I am sincerely grateful for each one of you.

With deepest appreciation,

Michael Alexander Beas

LAUREN BALCOMB

L AUREN BALCOMB, A NAME SYNONYMOUS WITH DEDICA-tion to the equestrian industry, was born in Sydney and has since become an integral figure in the Duffy's Forest community on the Northern Beaches of New South Wales, Australia. Beyond the shores of her Sydney upbringing lies Lamondale, her family's prestigious farm located in Wilberforce. It is within this idyllic haven that the Balcomb family breeds exceptional performance horses for dressage, showjumping, and eventing.

Balcomb's deep-rooted love for horses has spanned her entire life. Despite her parents' lack of equestrian background, her mother's enduring adoration for horses inspired a fire within her own heart. Horses, it seems, coursed through her veins, as evidenced by her lineage - a great grandfather who once graced the racecourses as a jockey and a granduncle who owned the legendary racehorse, Luskin Star.

At the tender age of five, Balcomb embarked on her equestrian journey, commencing her riding lessons with unwavering determination. By the age of seven, she had found her way to the Pony Club, savoring every moment spent in the saddle. The year of her twelfth birthday marked a significant milestone - an entry into her first event, solidifying her commitment to the art of horsemanship.

Upon completing her formal education, Balcomb stood at a crossroads, faced with the decision to pursue a conventional academic path, or follow the equestrian world that was calling her. With unwavering conviction, she chose the latter, embracing a life dedicated to her riding career. In 2008, an opportunity presented itself - a six-week sojourn in the United States, training under the esteemed guidance of equestrian luminaries Phillip Dutton and Boyd Martin. This eye-opening experience cemented Balcomb's resolve, kindling the desire to return to the United States and explore the vast horizons of equestrian excellence.

Throughout her illustrious career, Balcomb has nurtured and honed her craft, skillfully managing a string of up to twelve horses at a time. Beyond her personal endeavors, she also welcomed the opportunity to work with horses in need of schooling, leveraging her expertise to transform them into exceptional equine partners.

However, amidst the tapestry of Balcomb's remarkable journey, one horse stands as a testament to the bond between rider and steed—the horse that would forever etch its name upon her heart. Kootoomootoo, a true gem of equine majesty, emerged as the "one in a million horse" that graced her life with unbridled joy and an abundance of victories. Together, they triumphed over countless obstacles, emerging victorious in an array of prestigious competitions, and carving their names into the chronicles of equestrian history.

Today, Balcomb's unwavering dedication to equestrian excellence continues to drive her forward. With a wealth of experience, a deep-rooted passion, and an unyielding commitment to her craft, she stands poised at the precipice of new horizons, eager to embrace future triumphs. Lauren's remarkable journey serves as an inspiration to aspiring equestrians around the world, a testament to the transformative power of perseverance, passion, and an unshakeable bond between human and horse.

~~✺~~ LOUIS ✺~~

AROUND CHRISTMAS OF 1994 MY FAMILY HAD JUST moved to five acres from the inner city and there were some horses that were already boarding at our farm. I was horse mad, so Christmas day I went outside and there was a yearling that my parents had rescued. We called him Louis. He was there with a big red bow wrapped around him, and that was my first pony.

He was only a yearling but I'd been taking some riding lessons at a farm down the road from ours. I didn't own my own saddle or bridle, but I did have a helmet and a halter and a leg rope. So I decided to try to break him in myself and I would get on him bareback and ride him. He was more like a family pet than a competition horse. We kept trying to gift Louis to other people because he was still a stallion and he quite liked all of the mares that we had. He was a very naughty boy. He was a miniature Shetland; a tiny little thing, but with a lot of spunk. So we kept trying to gift him to people and he kept finding his way back to us. He passed away in the field one night and it was a very sad day. He was part of the family for a very long time. He lived to about 20 years of age.

My next pony was another paint called Prince. He was about 11.2 hands tall. We grew up doing Pony Club. I did jumping, eventing, and playing sporting mountain games on him. He was a great horse. He definitely started my love for three day eventing, which was what I predominantly did until my mid-twenties. He was just a really sweet horse. He had a lot of experience doing different disciplines.

When I was 12 years old, we bought a very good horse from Boyd Martin, who had bred a horse called Kootoomootoo. We bought him as a four-year-old. I was quite young being 12 and him being four, but that was really when I started my eventing career. I made the Australian Young Rider teams and won Young Rider of the Year multiple times with him. I also represented Australia on him. He was a pretty special three day horse.

Verdini D'Houtveld Z was really my transition into the show-jumping world here. I actually bought him in Europe when he was six years old. Sharn's business partner called him and said, "Hey, Sharn, I've got a really nice six year old that's probably going to be a good three day horse. He's got lots of blood, he's beautiful, and he jumps nicely. I think your girlfriend, Lauren, would really like him." So I bought him and he did some three day events and then we realized he was going to be too good of a jumper to be a three day horse. So then I had really decided I'd wanted to pursue show jumping and he was the horse that made that transition. He was my horse for my first time on a Nations Cup team representing Australia.

I produced him to the Grand Prix level and then when I was pregnant, Sharn started riding him. Unfortunately, I had to have a year off riding, so I told Sharn he better start riding him a little bit. And then he qualified to go to the Tokyo Olympics. He didn't end up taking him, but by then I had started riding him again. And then I represented Australia in the Nation's Cup team in Wellington this year. We were shortlisted for the World

Equestrian Games for Australia. Now the aim is to hopefully be looking at Paris next year. He's a very special horse.

Growing up, now that I look back at it, my parents weren't horsey at all. My mom adored horses, but they had no idea what they were doing and they went to a rescue place and they rescued this yearling pony, and of course he turned out to be a stallion and it was the most inappropriate first pony probably for a four year old child. But it made me tough. I did a lot of bareback riding and with a halter and fell off a lot, but I loved it. Every step you take on every horse has a big imprint.

Get Interactive
https://www.instagram.com/_mooie_/
Click / Scan the QR Code Below

JENNIFER BAUERSACHS

Photo Courtesy Shawn McMillen

JENNIFER BAUERSACHS, A NAME THAT RESONATES WITH EX-
cellence in the equestrian world, is the proud owner and
operator of Spring Hill Farm in Frenchtown, New Jersey.
Together with her husband, Rolf, she has built a haven
for young horses, focusing on their training as high-level, winning hunters and jumpers. The farm, known far and wide, has
earned a stellar reputation for producing champions and grand
champions in the professional, amateur, and junior hunter divisions at renowned shows such as the Washington International
Horse Show, Pennsylvania National, Hampton Classic, Old Salem Farm, and the illustrious Devon Horse Show and Country
Fair.

Within the competitive realm of equestrian sports, Bauersachs
has achieved numerous milestones that have solidified her status as a top-tier rider. Among her many triumphs, the Capital
Challenge 2021 holds a special place. Mounted on the talented
Blink, owned by the esteemed Lee Kellogg Sadrian, Bauersachs
displayed her exceptional skills and undeniable bond with her
horse. Together, they conquered the ring, leaving their mark on
the hearts of spectators and etching their names into the record
books.

The year 2022 brought forth a wave of victories for Bauersachs
at the Winter Equestrian Festival (WEF). Guiding Another Love
with finesse and precision, she claimed the championship title in
the highly competitive High-Performance Conformation Hunter division. Their success extended beyond a single category,
as they emerged triumphant in both the model and under saddle classes. The duo's expertise was further showcased in the
esteemed E.R. Mische Grand Hunter Ring, where they secured
two first-place finishes, a second, and a fourth, solidifying their
status as true champions.

While Bauersachs' list of accomplishments is extensive, there
are two moments that hold a special place in her heart. The first
is her distinction as the Leading Lady Rider at the revered Devon
Horse Show and Country Fair, a prestigious title that highlights
not only her exceptional talent but also her unwavering dedica-

tion and hard work. The second moment of immense pride came with her crowning as the Grand Champion in the Green Hunters at the esteemed Washington International Horse Show. These cherished achievements serve as a testament to Bauersachs' relentless pursuit of excellence and her ability to achieve greatness in the world of equestrian sports.

Bauersachs and Spring Hill Farm have become synonymous with success, passion, and a commitment to nurturing young horses into champions. Their journey continues to inspire and captivate the equestrian community, leaving an indelible mark on the sport and showcasing the remarkable heights that can be reached through dedication and an unwavering love for the noble equine partner.

❦ HARMONY ❧

I WAS ALWAYS A HORSE-CRAZY GIRL, BUT MY PARENTS KNEW nothing about horses, so it took a while to convince them to even let me take a riding lesson. Finally, my mom gave in and said I could get a horse. The very first horse that I went to look at was owned by a friend of my sister's. The horse was in their backyard and her name was Harmony. She was a chestnut mare.

I was 10 or 11 years old at the time when I tried her. The funny thing was that when I was trying her, I couldn't stop her, so everyone made a human chain which the horse broke through. Finally, I got her to stop. My mom was terrified and wouldn't let me get the horse, but I told her, "She's perfect! I love her." We ended up buying Harmony for $500 dollars and we got her vetted for another $50 which was basically to say her heart was still beating and her lungs were good. Harmony was at my uncle's farm, where he kept Shetland ponies.

I had her for a few years and then I decided I wanted to jump.

At my uncle's farm, I used to show the Shetland ponies that he had in hand. '*You must make them park out and they must put their knees up and down,*' he would say. I did all of that stuff with my uncle until I finally started to ride English.

My mom caught me jumping fences out in our field and realized I would need to take lessons. Right down the road from our house was a farm, so I brought my pony there and started taking lessons.

I showed mostly locally in the beginning, but I got to show at Devon and the National Horse Show also. At the time I had a good horse named Drafty who I thought had all the scope of the world. I showed him through the juniors and the amateurs and won a lot with him.

My story is a little bit different from most. My goal in the show ring today is to make sure that my horses are well enough so that the clients can ride them. I'm more worried about their success. That's my success too. You know, you want to be proud of the horses that you sell.

I have been fortunate to ride so many wonderful horses and have had success. The most interesting part of my career is that I was someone who didn't have a lot of money and was able to work and be recognized for the hard work. For example, I just wouldn't leave the barn; I was constantly sweeping or watering. I just made myself a fixture in the barn. It became evident that was what I wanted to do and really gave me some opportunities, and eventually that is how I became a better rider.

I feel like early on, I lived in the barn, and I didn't get paid, and I was happy to do whatever was asked of me. There were plenty of times I had to go fix the fences. I mucked all the stalls for three years. I did it all by myself and swept the barn constantly to keep up with the standard that we wanted for the barn.

It was my job to clean all the tack and do all the grooming and flip the horses. Now, I can do almost everything that needs to be done in this business, and I feel very fortunate that I can do all that. That's not the case for a lot of people - they just want to ride. I wanted a good foundation too for myself also and so that is my advice to others to follow and model.

There is a lot more to this sport than just riding. Riding is a privilege and doing all the other stuff like taking care of the horses, mucking their stalls, learning everything that you need to do to take care of their legs and how to take care of all the equipment just makes you appreciate these animals so much more. You're never going to go wrong when you are making choices about something if you're putting the horse first. It's always for the love of the horse.

Get Interactive
Click / Scan the QR Code Below

VICTORIA COLVIN

VICTORIA "TORI" COLVIN IS AN ESTEEMED RIDER AND trainer who has established her own company, Victoria Colvin, LLC, following a highly successful junior career. Based in Wellington, FL, Colvin's business provides clients with the opportunity to train under the guidance of a renowned show rider/trainer and compete in top-notch horse shows across North America. Colvin also offers services for sourcing, developing, and selling exceptional young show horses.

Colvin's journey to success began with remarkable achievements in her childhood. She earned an unprecedented record of five Best Child Rider titles at the renowned Devon Horse Show and Country Fair, a testament to her exceptional talent and dedication. Moreover, she accumulated numerous victories in Junior Hunter and Equitation competitions across the country, showcasing her versatility and mastery in various arenas.

Colvin's prowess in the hunter discipline is exemplified by her unprecedented success in the International Hunter Derbies, where she has emerged as the champion on numerous occasions. Additionally, she has triumphed an incredible six times in the prestigious $100,000 WCHR Peter Wetherill Palm Beach Hunter Spectacular, a feat unmatched by any other rider, solidifying her status as a force to be reckoned with in the hunter ring.

✣ BUSTER BROWN ✣

MY FIRST PONY WAS NAMED BUSTER BROWN BEcause he was a very faintly brown medium pony. He was the best pony and he started me off getting comfortable riding.

We got connected with Buster Brown through my mother being friends with his owner. My mom rode dressage and her friend that owned him said that he would be a good pony for me to start on because I was a little nervous riding. He turned out to be a good nerve-breaker. I believe we had him for about four years. He was older when we got him, but he started me on trotting and the basics of everything. He taught me probably everything I know and gave me the confidence that I have now.

My next pony I had was named King of the Road. He was a great pony and I showed him in the Short Stirrups and the Children's Hunter divisions.

My next pony after that was Ballou, who kind of started my career. At first, we had him on trial and he didn't know very much so we were not going to buy him. But he was in a paddock while we had him on trial for a week and he got hurt. And then we had to buy him. We're very lucky that we did because he ended up being an incredible pony. He won at Pony Finals. He did a lot of great stuff. He was beautiful, and a good jumper. He won a lot of things with me and then also after I had him, with a couple of other riders as well. He won a couple of championships at the fall Indoor shows like Washington Horse Show and Capital Challenge Horse Show. Now he is in Virginia. Betsee Parker bought him. He is basically retired but still does little stuff, such as Leadline, in Virginia.

I left ponies around the age of nine or 10 because I got too big. Then I started Junior Hunters when I was 10 or 11. The first horse I showed in the junior ranks was named Leader. After that my first Junior Hunter was World Time. I did him in the Derby Finals when I was 12 and I was fourth in that show.

There have been many horses that have been part of my career. Nowadays, I have 22 horses in my barn but they're not mine; they belong to clients. They all rotate. I show them all and then I have a couple outside client horses that I show as well.

My advice to up-and-coming riders is to keep practicing and always have your spirits up and always have a good time. I always have a good time. Everything has always been fun for me. It was never hard. It wasn't ever like a job. It was always a fun activity to do, and I always made fun of it.

Get Interactive
https://www.victoriacolvin.com
Click / Scan the QR Code Below

DANIEL GEITNER

Photo courtesy of Andrew Ryback Photography

A LIFELONG EQUESTRIAN, DANIEL GEITNER'S JOURNEY in the world of horses has been filled with passion, dedication, and countless achievements. From his early days with ponies to owning his own stable in Aiken, South Carolina, Geitner's love for riding and competing has become a family affair. Together with his wife, Cathy, and their talented daughter, Lilly, the Geitner family has created a legacy of success that continues to shine.

Looking at the results page on their stable's website, one can see a string of recent victories for Geitner. Among his recent accomplishments, one stands out prominently—the $20,000 Golden Ocala Golf & Equestrian Club 3'6"- 3'9" Hunter Derby. Teaming up with Easy Money, owned by Laura Cramer, he showcased his expertise and finesse, earning an impressive overall score of 185 and securing the well-deserved victory. Additionally, Geitner's mastery was on full display as he rode Don Stewart's Story Hour to win the $15,000 UF Veterinary Hospital 3' Open Hunter Derby.

Reflecting on his illustrious career, Geitner estimates that he has won more than 50 Grand Prix events, perhaps even reaching the remarkable milestone of 70-80 victories. These accomplishments, however, trace back to the beginning, the days when his journey started with his first pony.

M Y FIRST PONY WAS A LITTLE SHETLAND MARE named Silly Sally. We got her from a local riding school that had gone out of business and she was a real sweetheart; a very easy pony. I rode her Western and did costume classes and went trail riding and all kinds of fun stuff with her.

I rode her for about a year, and by then she got a little old and wasn't quite sound enough to do all the cowboying I wanted to do, so we retired her. Silly Sally lived out her days on our farm.

My next pony was a little red roan mare named Puppy Chow and she was a tough one. She was really strong. We thought she was going to be my show pony, but she was difficult and she would stop at the jumps if I didn't ride her perfectly. She would bite, kick, and stop at the jumps and I've never seen anything stop so fast, and she would canter down there like she was going to jump. We hired a couple of local professionals to come ride her and see if they could get her jumping and nobody had much luck; not many people could hang onto her. My dad ended up selling her for $100 at a flea market.

My next pony was probably my first show pony and her name was Shenandoah Glitter and she came from Phil DeVita. She was a great medium pony and she was such a nice mover. I think I started her in Short Stirrup and went all the way into the Medium Pony Hunters with her. She lived out her days on our farm also. Pat Dodson was my coach then and he found that pony for me along with Keith Hastings. They also found my next pony named Playing for Keeps. He was a Thoroughbred/ Quarter Horse and real quality, but he had a lead change that was a little funny. It taught me the importance of properly asking for changes and flat work and he helped me take the next step in my education.

When I moved on to horses, my first horse was named Bingo, and he was my Equitation and Junior Hunter horse.

Eventually, I went to boarding school for a couple of years up in Connecticut and then went to college.

After college I started out on my own, rented a little barn in Laurinburg, NC for a year and came to a horse show in Aiken in April. I loved it and stayed - never went home. I met my wife in college and she graduated a year before I did. She was teaching at Chatham Hall in Virginia at the time. When I moved to Aiken, I called her and asked her if she wanted to join me and she did.

Now our daughter, Lilly, has been riding since she was a little kid. We've always had her on ponies. And she's ridden a lot of different horses and ponies, like a typical professional's kid. She gets them going good and then they get sold. That was a little tough for her at first, but she's gotten used to it now. We started a little savings account for her, and every time we sell one, we make sure to put some more money in there. She's getting old enough to understand that now. She's going up to the Junior

Hunters and Junior Jumpers and Equitation and doing a little bit of everything and she recently even won at Pony Finals.

I want to take a moment to say something about the horse business, because it's a great business. I really love riding new horses, riding different horses, getting to know each horse, and figuring out what makes them tick. These horses have given us so much! I've been able to lead a great life. It doesn't feel like work. It still feels like a hobby to me.

I'd also like to say something to the young professionals. Work as hard as you can and don't have much pride. Don't be afraid to muck stalls, wrap your horses, and do all the little things. Pay attention whether you're at a show or in the schooling area or at a clinic or riding a horse for somebody else. Keep your eyes and ears open. There's free lessons to be had out there. Whether it's a vet, a blacksmith, a braider, or a groom, you can learn something from everybody.

Get Interactive

Click / Scan the QR Code Below

MIMI GOCHMAN

Photo Courtesy Kind Media

A T THE YOUNG AGE OF 19, MIMI GOCHMAN HAS AL-
ready made quite an impressionable mark in the
equestrian world, earning widespread recognition
and admiration for her outstanding riding abilities.
Her exceptional list of awards and accolades serves as a testament to her talent and dedication.

Gochman achieved remarkable success by earning the Individual Bronze at the FEI Youth Equestrian Games in 2022, demonstrating her ability to compete at the highest level on an international stage. Her noteworthy talent was further acknowledged
when she was awarded the prestigious Lionel Guerrand-Hermès
Trophy by the U.S. Equestrian Team Foundation in the same
year, cementing her status as an exceptional young equestrian.

In 2021, Gochman showcased her skill and determination by se-
curing the gold medal in the highly competitive $25,000 Young
Rider Individual Final at the Gotham North FEI North American
Youth Jumping Championships. This impressive achievement
placed her among a select group of riders who represented the
United States on an international level.

Throughout her career, Gochman has consistently excelled in
various events, capturing significant victories along the way.
In 2017, she triumphed in the prestigious WCHR Spectacular
Hunter Night at the Winter Equestrian Festival, solidifying her
reputation as a top-class hunter rider. Additionally, in 2019, she
emerged victorious in the $25,000 USHJA National Hunter Der-
by at the Brandywine Horse Show.

Gochman comes from an equestrian family, and she deeply ap-
preciates the unwavering support she receives from her parents,
Becky and David. Their encouragement and guidance have
played a vital role in her success, serving as a solid foundation
for her growth as a rider. Every lesson learned in the barn or
show ring and every successful moment celebrated all started
with one special pony years ago.

MY SISTER, SOPHIE, AND I SHARED OUR FIRST PONY, named Lacey. She was a large, older gray pony, and she only did the Leadline classes with us. We learned how to walk and trot on her, but she really didn't jump. She was very, very sweet. I have fond memories of her. What's funny is that she was so big, and we were really small, but she was wonderful. I remember we brought her to Devon, and she did the Leadline class there. I was fourth on her and we had lots of great memories with her.

My parents had learned about Lacey being available through our trainer at the time, Peter Pletcher. Lacey was known to be a sweet, docile pony; a good first pony for kids to play around on, make mistakes on, and learn how to ride. My sister and I rode her together around the same time. We also got another pony, named Dolphin around the same time, but he jumped and was a bit younger than Lacey.

Lacey retired after we finished learning on her. She was older and we wanted her to have a good, happy life, so she retired in Texas at Peter Pletcher's farm. Then I started showing a pony called Tinker. She was a strawberry roan. We still had Dolphin, who was known as Farnley Dolphin, and we did them in the cross rails classes and up to the Small Pony Hunter division. They were amazing. They were our first ponies and I remember learning how to canter on them. Our trainer used to get on the back of the pony with us because he was tiny, and he would teach us how to canter and do lead changes. Both ponies won tons of classes, and they went on for quite a while after we were finished with them.

Neither of them went to Pony Finals with us though. The first time I went to Pony Finals was when I was six years old. I went on a pony named Jack, also known as Embellished. I remember I fell off in the hack, so I had to go first in the jumping portion, but we got around the ring and he was good, so it was a great first experience. I learned a lot and earned a sportsmanship award that day.

I rode ponies for about five years; I guess I was eleven when I stopped doing ponies. My mom had a few hunters that she let us ride around on.

My first horse was named Romance. He was a big bay, and he was beautiful, and a good mover, but he was a little bit nippy around the stalls. Still, he was amazing and I did the Children's Hunter division, then the 3'3" Junior Hunters, and then ended up doing 3'6" Junior Hunters on him too. Now he is retired but he was my first horse.

I did Junior Hunters for quite a while. One of my most known hunters was Cosmic, known as Evermore, and I did the Small Junior Hunters for quite a while with him. He won a lot of big championships with me at Devon and at Indoors before he retired a few years ago, and that's about when I stopped showing hunters.

Then I did jumpers for mostly two years, and then my mom, just for the last two years, let me ride her hunter, Catch Me, who's a well-known hunter. My mom won everything on him and she let me compete on him for the last two years. We had an amazing time. And Scott Stewart showed him for a bit also and got a 100 score on him once. He's a very special boy. My mom competes on him in the 3'3" Amateur Owner Hunters. He wins the championship almost every single weekend with her, and he loves his job.

My first jumper's name was Sundance. Her name was Sunny in the barn, and she was amazing. She could turn tight and just jump everything. She was the fastest little horse ever. My sister and I both shared her a bit. We got into the jumpers around the same time as we started doing the hunter divisions around 11 and 12 and we just had a bunch of fun.

We did the little jumpers, and Sunny brought us up to the 3'6" jumpers. I've continued to do jumpers throughout the rest of my career. I've had an amazing time. Now I have my core team of jumpers, and I'm starting to jump the Grand Prix and FEI classes, so I'm trying to move up a little bit and see how that goes. Also, I hope to compete still, while in college. On the longer school breaks, I'll have the opportunity to continue riding, but school is the priority. I plan to get a good education and still get to compete.

After college, I hope to keep competing and be on some championship teams. I will also pursue a job in a non-horse aspect and see what else there is out there, but I will definitely, always continue to compete at the highest level I can. Right now, I'm grateful for the ability to do this at such a high level, so I hope to continue this in the future.

My advice for the young riders coming up is to love on your horses and remember the joy of this sport. It's a hard sport and it can be challenging at times, but don't ever give up and keep working hard. Also, watch what your idols are doing. Watch the top riders and see what they're doing and what you can change about your riding or change about your program and always aspire to do better.

Get Interactive
http://www.baxterhill.com/riders-1
Click / Scan the QR Code Below

DANNY ROBERTSHAW

Photo Courtesy Anne Gittins

DANNY ROBERTSHAW IS A LEGENDARY HUNTER RIDER and trainer, widely recognized for his exceptional skills and contributions to the equestrian community. He is not only a highly accomplished athlete but also holds esteemed positions within the United States Equestrian Federation (USEF) and the United States Hunter Jumper Association (USHJA). As a testament to his expertise, Robertshaw is licensed as a judge with a distinguished "R" rating by the USEF.

During his competitive years, Robertshaw achieved unprecedented success by becoming the first rider to secure championships in the Regular Working Hunters at prestigious events such as the Devon Horse Show, the Pennsylvania National Horse Show, the Washington International Horse Show, the National Horse Show, and the Royal Winter Fair, all in a single season. His notable achievements were made possible by his exceptional partnership with remarkable hunters like Lestat, Parody, Silent Runner, and numerous other talented equine companions.

Presently, Robertshaw and his partner, the esteemed hunter trainer, Ron Danta, co-own and operate Beaver River Farm, located in the picturesque town of Camden, South Carolina. Additionally, they maintain a training base in Wellington, Florida, where they continue to hone the skills of both riders and horses in the hunter discipline. Beyond their equestrian pursuits, Danny and Ron are the proud founders of Danny & Ron's Rescue, an organization dedicated to rescuing and rehoming dogs in need. Through their unwavering commitment, the rescue has successfully facilitated the adoption of over 14,000 dogs, positively impacting countless lives.

Robertshaw's lifelong passion for animals began with a pony that he first rode in his pajamas, marking the start of a remarkable journey that has brought him immense success in the equestrian world. His dedication to horsemanship, combined with his profound love for animals, continues to inspire and make a lasting impact on both the equestrian and animal rescue communities.

～⊛ READY GO ⊛～

MY JOURNEY IN THE EQUESTRIAN WORLD BEGAN with a pony named Ready Go, and it was a momentous Christmas when he became my very own. It turns out, my sister had orchestrated a secret plan with her boyfriend and in the dark of night on Christmas Eve, they brought Ready Go to our backyard, ensuring a delightful surprise for me. On Christmas morning, I heard laughter and initially thought my family was opening presents without me. Curiosity got the better of me, and I rushed downstairs to investigate. Opening the back door, I was greeted by the sight of my sister happily mounted on my new pony.

Without hesitation, I knew I had to ride him immediately, even if it meant venturing out in my pajamas. Picture this: I lived in a regular neighborhood, complete with backyard clotheslines. Yet, there I was, galloping up and down the yards, deftly maneuvering around the clotheslines, barefoot and clad in my pajamas, with a small Western saddle and bridle adorning my pony.

Ready Go, a black and white Shetland Welsh cross, brought immense joy into my life. What stands out in my mind about him is that I rode him Western style. Back then, I didn't possess an English saddle, but I had observed my sister posting during her rides. With no knowledge of how people typically rode Western horses, I simply imitated my sister's posting motion. Little did I know that my unconventional style would raise eyebrows. Nonetheless, I posted away in my little Western saddle, oblivious to any perceived anomaly. At that point, I had never been to a horse show, apart from accompanying my sister when she rode a few ponies for a local lady. Although I had witnessed the events, I lacked the understanding to fully comprehend them.

As time passed, I outgrew Ready Go, and the lady who owned the barn where I rode had a pony who was originally purchased for her niece, Amy. The pony proved too frisky for Amy's liking as he reared up, causing her to lose confidence. One day, while riding in the front lot, a couple drove by and saw me with Ready Go. They had a young boy with them and inquired if they could buy my pony. It was a daunting prospect to consider parting with him, but I accepted their contact information. Later, I spoke with the lady who owned the farm, and she advised me that I had nearly outgrown his size and that he needed another young rider to train. She suggested that it might be time for me to move up to a larger mount since Amy would not be riding her pony anymore.

As much as it pained me to let him go, I knew it was for the best. We called the interested buyers, and my $150 pony sold for $275. The silver lining was that I still had the opportunity to see him every day and kept track of him throughout his life. He lived until the ripe old age of 36, albeit nearly blind. He had truly lived a good life.

Next on my equestrian journey came King B, and I unknowingly took on the role of teaching him to jump. It never occurred to me that I was imparting any knowledge; I simply knew that I wanted to jump, and so we did. Shortly thereafter, I acquired my first

41

English saddle, which happened to be a racehorse saddle. It was comically oversized, extending about two feet beyond what was suitable for me, lacking proper flaps on the sides. I would often slide up and down in it, and I remember overhearing the lady who taught riding in town comment, "That little boy slides in the saddle like it's a wash tub." I couldn't help but feel indignant upon hearing that remark!

Eventually, my first horse show arrived, and I believed I had dressed impeccably for the occasion. Clad in a small black coat, a matching bow tie, a dainty black hat, and a hunt bridle with a curved bit, I felt ready to conquer the world. It was then that I learned about snaffles and realized they presented a more polished appearance. I promptly switched to a snaffle bridle, although I likely left it a few holes too loose. Nevertheless, King B was an incredible pony who never let me down.

As time passed, I outgrew King B as well, and he was purchased by some individuals for $600. With the funds from his sale, I bought my first horse at the age of 12. She was only 22 months old and had been ridden just twice in Western tack. Despite her youth and limited training, I fearlessly rode her, and she proved to be a gentle teacher, never causing me harm. She taught me countless invaluable lessons, and I thought she was magnificent.

She excelled in trail classes, effortlessly outperforming the Western horses. Additionally, the hunter hack classes of that era involved an extended trot, a hand gallop, and a halt. I practiced the extended trot along the roadside near a golf course on my way to the park where I conducted my flat work. My horse eventually developed a trot akin to that of a standardbred, but I could sit deeply in the saddle and utilize my leg to subtly guide her mouth, prompting her to shift into an incredible gear and soar effortlessly. Our performances consistently led to victories, despite her average talent. She possessed an extraordinary ability to retain and execute what we practiced.

Get Interactive
https://dannyronsrescue.org
Click / Scan the QR Code Below

HAVENS SCHATT

Photo Courtesy Andrew Ryback

HAVENS SCHATT IS A HIGHLY ACCOMPLISHED HUNTER rider and trainer, whose success can be traced back to her impressive junior career. Following her junior years, she honed her skills under the guidance of renowned trainer Tom Wright for an impressive nine-year period before embarking on her own professional journey. Together with her husband Frederic Commissaire, she established Milestone Farm, a thriving equestrian enterprise located in Lexington, KY.

Throughout her career, Schatt has consistently emerged as a dominant force in the hunter ring, securing numerous championships at prestigious horse shows such as the illustrious Devon Horse Show and all of the fall Indoor competitions. Her exceptional performances have also resulted in multiple victories in hunter derbies, further solidifying her status as a top-class competitor.

Among her notable achievements, Schatt holds the impressive distinction of being a two-time winner of the World Equestrian Center (WEC) Hunter Derby in the 3'6" to 3'9" division. This esteemed accomplishment speaks volumes about her skill, precision, and ability to navigate challenging derby courses.

Schatt's remarkable journey in the equestrian world can be traced back to her early experiences, particularly her fond memories of riding a pony that left a lasting impression on her. These formative experiences ignited her passion for the sport and set the stage for her subsequent achievements as a rider and trainer.

SATIN

MY FIRST PONY WAS A BROWN AND WHITE PINTO named Satin. She did everything I wanted to do; drive the cart, ride Western, ride English and she taught me how to jump. She did everything. We had her for five or six years, then she retired and stayed with my aunt, who took care of her.

From there, we had a pony named Rhythm and Rhyme. She was a green pony, so my mom broke her in so I could ride her. We did the Short Stirrup division at Marion Saddle Club in Ocala, Florida while she was still a green pony.

The first pony to take me to the Indoor Finals was named Center Shot. She was a very small medium pony, but we won everything. After that first year at Indoors, we sold her to a client of Jack Towell's named Amanda Lyerly, who's now a great professional. That little pony has two pretty good professionals on her list.

Then I moved up to horses and went to ride with Don Stewart. I was probably 11, and I was still tiny, but we got a horse that could do Children's Hunters and Junior Hunter divisions on. His name was Super Shot. I took him to my first Medal Finals. It was a little over his head, but he tried and he did it. And from there, I was lucky enough to be riding with Don Stewart and got to ride sale horses. I even got to ride the most perfect horse named Plain Brown Wrapper. He was my first real horse for Junior Hunters at Indoors and he was a great horse.

I was champion at Harrisburg on him and I guess my biggest claim to fame on him is we won the Junior Hunter Winter Stake at Harrisburg and we retired the trophy. Thank goodness I didn't know it was that important. I just went in there and rode and won and then we retired the trophy. I believe now they don't have that particular class at Harrisburg anymore, but I think the Junior Stake that they have is still the Plain Brown Wrapper Challenge.

I only rode that horse one year; Don Stewart leased him out to a lot of his clients and each year he had a new rider. And I'm not exactly sure how that happened. I started riding him halfway through the year. I don't remember who rode him before because I just remember thinking, "Oh my gosh, I get to ride Plain Brown Wrapper!" It was quite a treat because I was only about 14 years old. I was young to be able to ride such a great horse. And then from there I mostly rode sales horses for Don the rest of my junior career.

Then I went to the University of Florida and one summer while I was still in college, I went to work for Turtle Lane Farm. I did that for nine months and while I was there, I met Tom Wright. He called one day and asked if I would be interested in coming to work for him. I said, "I'm still not finished with school yet, but I'll come for three months and see how it goes."

Then I stayed there for nine and half years!

We had Lindner Family there and they had so many great horses like Straight Man and High Hearts and it was fun. The Lindner children won as much as I won, and it was a great run. But all things need to change. I met my husband, Fred Commissaire, during that period and then we started our own business in 2000.

It's amazing to think about all the wonderful things that have happened. Now that I am further along in my career, I have some advice for riders coming up now.

If you are a young rider, take heart. There are so many ups and downs in this business. You have to take the good with the bad. For sure I've been lucky enough to ride great horses, be associated with great people, and have great experiences. Some of the events that come to mind include being champion at Devon in the Small and Large Junior Hunters and winning the Medal and Maclay there the same year, as well as being Best Child Rider when I was young in my career.

My advice to young riders is to keep in mind there are going to be good days and there are going to be bad days. There have been many days when I've been riding my horse, and nothing was going right, and I would just say, "tomorrow's another day."

Also, I've had quite a few good mentors along the way. I am grateful when I think of all these people that gave their time to come to our little backyard with me in my bathing suit and shorts and chaps. And as soon as the riding lesson was over, the chaps and the pony went away. (I washed her off in the field in the pool.) I was very lucky to be able to have the ponies in my backyard and for my mom to know the people she knows. (She had a great career in the hunter world, and equitation world when she was a Junior.) I always say I was fed with a silver spoon, but at the same time I knew I had to take those opportunities and work hard to get where I am. You can have that opportunity, but if you don't take advantage of it, it won't help you. Never give up. Keep trying. There's always something to learn. Don't ever think you know at all. And the horses really can talk to you if you are patient with them and let them speak. They'll tell you what they're ready for and what they're not. And you know, I always say Rome wasn't built in a day.

Get Interactive
Click / Scan the QR Code Below

WILL SIMPSON

Photo Courtesy Andrew Ryback Photography

WILL SIMPSON IS A RENOWNED EQUESTRIAN WHO gained widespread recognition for his remarkable achievements as a member of the U.S. Show Jumping Team at the 2008 Summer Olympics in Beijing, China. Alongside his talented teammates, Simpson played an instrumental role in securing a team gold medal for the United States, solidifying his status as an exceptional rider.

Currently based in Ocala, Florida, Simpson has been actively involved in the equestrian community for many years. From 1998 to 2008, he held the esteemed position of President of the West Coast Active Riders, where he demonstrated his commitment to fostering camaraderie and excellence among fellow equestrians. With a strong belief in the importance of giving back, Simpson also served on the board of the Compton Junior Posse, a program dedicated to coaching underprivileged, inner-city children in equestrian pursuits during its active years. Through his involvement, he positively impacted the lives of numerous young individuals, igniting their passion for horses and providing them with valuable guidance.

Acknowledged as a prominent figure in the equestrian community, Simpson's leadership extends beyond his local engagements. He served as a board member of the North American Riders Group, contributing his expertise and insights to the advancement of the sport. Moreover, he assumed the esteemed position of Chairman of the High-Performance Committee of the United States Equestrian Federation (USEF) for a significant number of years, where he played a crucial role in shaping the direction and development of high-performance equestrian programs.

Throughout his illustrious career, Simpson has proudly represented the United States in five World Cup finals, showcasing his extraordinary talent on the international stage. With an impressive record of over 75 Grand Prix victories, he has consistently demonstrated his mastery of the sport and his ability to excel in highly competitive events. As a testament to his enduring passion and dedication, Simpson continues to actively compete and showcase his skills in various show jumping competitions across the United States and Canada.

Simpson's contributions to the equestrian world extend far beyond his personal accomplishments. His unwavering commitment to the sport, his involvement in various organizations, and his continuous pursuit of excellence have left an indelible mark on the equestrian community. He is recognized not only for his extraordinary achievements but also for his selfless dedication to fostering the growth and success of equestrian athletes at all levels.

❧ OLD JOE ❧

THE FIRST PONY EXPERIENCE I HAD WAS QUITE AN AD-
venture. It all began when my dad won two unbroke Welsh ponies in a raffle. My siblings and I were
beyond excited. We were shouting, "Let's go! Let's
go ride them!" We would have taken them to school if we were
allowed! However, our dad made a trade, and we ended up with
Old Joe, a Palomino pony who was likely around 15 years old.
All of my siblings, except my older sister who was allergic to
horses, had the opportunity to ride Old Joe. Mom and dad would
often get bored and head inside, leaving us with the pony. The
trainer would eventually get bored also and leave us to ride on
our own. But we didn't mind because we were having so much
fun.

As we grew more comfortable with Old Joe, we started jumping
a cross rail. But even that became monotonous after a while, so
we came up with a new idea. We began having fall off contests.
Yes, you heard that right! We would ride up to the cross rail, hurl
ourselves off the horse, and try to make the most dramatic fall.

Looking back, I realize it was good training, teaching us how to fall safely.

Eventually, we outgrew the fall off contests and decided to step up our jumping game. We progressed to a vertical, although it was only about a foot tall, the size of a five-gallon paint can. We thought we were really going for it. But poor Old Joe didn't quite make it over the jump. He tripped and fell on the other side, leaving us worried and running to get help. My parents came to the rescue, gave Old Joe a little boot in the belly, and he jumped right back up. Phew!

My dad asked us what happened, and I explained how we attempted the vertical and what unfolded. He then firmly said, "Well, don't ever do that again! Stick with the cross rail." Lesson learned.

Eventually, we said goodbye to Old Joe and welcomed King, a spirited horse who felt like a Ferrari compared to our previous pony. King had a roached mane that made him look like a majestic Trojan horse. We were particularly excited about him because the trainer shared a special trick with us. He instructed us to get to the far end of the ring, get King into a canter, lean forward, and say, "Run home!" We thought this was the coolest thing ever, believing King was incredibly well-trained. Little did we know, he was simply barn sour and would run straight for the gate upon hearing those words. We had been tricked, but it added an extra element of excitement to our rides.

After King, we welcomed Peanuts, a cost-effective horse who had retired from the racetrack. He was a little green but had a gentle nature. We had started riding him, and soon there was a horse show in Springfield, Illinois at the Illinois State Armory that caught our attention. There, we discovered a horse named Glenda Joe, and my dad decided to buy her. Glenda Joe turned out to be a remarkable jumper, winning four open jumpers and four junior jumpers at a small horse show in Taylorville, Illinois. We were proud to take her to the Indiana State Fair, where she once again triumphed in both junior jumpers and open jumpers.

As I reflect on my equestrian journey, I realize that there were many horses along the way. While my memory may drift at times, certain special moments with horses always stand out. One memory involves a horse that had some insecurities about jumping. To guide him, I held two dressage whips, using them to steer and encourage him. In a magical moment, he wanted to sell me out and stop at a jump, but with the whips guiding him, he mustered up the courage and successfully cleared the obstacle. It felt like an extraordinary connection, as if I had tapped into some mystical horse-whispering power. I never hit him with the whips; it was more about giving him the extra support and courage he needed. Moments like that are etched in my mind, reminding me of the incredible journey that began with two unbroke ponies my father won in a raffle.

Get Interactive
https://www.willsimpsonstables.com
Click / Scan the QR Code Below

AMANDA STEEGE

© ANDREW RYBACK 2022

Photo Courtesy Andrew Ryback

AMANDA STEEGE HAS MADE A REMARKABLE IMPACT ON the equestrian industry, most notably in the professional hunter divisions. Her equestrian journey began in Massachusetts, where she grew up in a family deeply involved in the hunter/jumper industry. Her parents, both instructors, worked at Saddle River Farm for Hank and Marion Hulick in Sterling, Massachusetts. As a junior rider, Steege achieved notable success in various disciplines, including Pony Hunters, Junior Hunters, and Equitation classes. She won the 1991 Massachusetts Medal Finals and participated in the esteemed Medal and Maclay Finals.

After completing her studies at Boston College, where she pursued a psychology degree, Steege wholeheartedly embraced her passion for horses and embarked on her journey as a professional equestrian, establishing Ashmeadow Farm as her own venture. Today, Steege divides her time between her Ocala, Florida and Califon, New Jersey bases, catering to a diverse clientele of both professional and amateur riders. Her students have achieved numerous titles along the East Coast, attesting to her exceptional training abilities. Additionally, Steege is recognized for her expertise in developing young horses.

Within the hunter/jumper arena, Steege has amassed an impressive array of victories and accomplishments. She has excelled in international derbies and has consecutively clinched the title of World Champion Hunter Rider for the northeast region multiple times. Perhaps her most recognized partner, the Belgian Warmblood owned by Cheryl Olsten, Lafitte De Muze has been a standout partner for Steege, earning prestigious titles such as the champion of the $50,000 National Horse Show Hunter Classic in 2019 and the victor of the $50,000 WCHR Professional Challenge at the Capital Challenge Horse Show in 2018. Lafitte De Muze was also awarded the esteemed 2019 WCHR Hunter of the Year, securing the illustrious Peter Wetherill Cup. Together, they have continued to secure top honors at a multitude of hunter derbies at the World Equestrian Center in Ocala, Florida.

❧ PEPPER ❧

MY FIRST PONY'S NAME WAS PEPPER. MY FATHER found him for me. We lived in Massachusetts when I was growing up, and my parents ran a horse farm called Red Acre Farm. At that time, my father was traveling to teach some kids nearby, and there was a pony in the front yard. Every day when he drove in and drove out, he saw it there. The pony was tied to a stake; not like he was being abused or anything, but they didn't have a fence, so they just tied this pony to a stake in the front yard. Finally, the fifth or sixth time he went there to teach the kids he asked about the pony, and they said that it didn't really have a job, so he became my first pony.

Pepper wasn't a show pony. He was more a beginners pony for teaching or play. Mostly he was good for teaching me how to trot and be on the lunge line and things like that. My sister and I both dragged him around to all the horse shows and he entertained us all day while my parents were working.

When it was time for me to move on to the next pony, something that I could ride more independently, my sister, Casey, took over Pepper. Pepper was not that great when he wasn't on the lead line, so she used to ride him a lot in the indoor ring. He was giving her a hard time one day and I thought I knew everything by then, so I told her I was going to get on him and train him for her! Keep in mind, I was probably six or seven at the most.

I got on Pepper in the indoor. It was summertime, and we rode him in the indoor because he didn't steer that well. The doors were open and there were four-by-fours across the ends just to keep the horses inside. My sister would ride Pepper around in there, and sometimes Pepper would run under the four-by-fours. My sister was little and very flexible, and when she knew he was going to do that, she would just lay back and go right under. So when I got on him, I was convinced that I was going to train him not to do that for her, which did not go so great. Pepper made the same move with me. He trotted once or twice around, and then he exited the ring. But I sat up straight and just busted the board in half with my chest.

He didn't fall and I didn't fall off. My dad said it was like Wonder Woman busting through the four by four at the edge of the ring.

My next pony after that was a little white pony named Ballerina that I did in the Short Stirrup and then shortly after that I had a pony named Quiz Kid. That was a famous pony. He had already done Pony Finals and all of that. He was older by the time I got him, and he was a great pony. He was the pony that I really got to start competing on. He didn't do lead changes though - he just refused. So, I am lead change obsessed now!

My next pony was a large pony named Mooney and I got him when he was a four-year-old. I showed Mooney a lot. Then he got handed down to my sister. That's how we did it. When I was finished with a pony, it would go to my sister. And then when my sister was finished with it, it would get leased out to other kids in the barn. And then when they were finished with it, it would go into my mom's riding school because my mom, still to this day, teaches about 70 kids a week at her farm in Massachusetts.

We didn't ever really sell our ponies. Once they came into the family, they stayed there and had a good life.

Next, I had a horse who was small, flea bitten, gray, and not a fancy mover. He was seen and tried and sort of passed over but the horse that I had to ride at the time passed away from colic. So I got Spanky. The woman who owned Spanky let me show him at the local horse show one weekend in the Children's Hunters and I was champion. She let me show him some more and eventually that became the main horse that I showed. We did the Small Junior Hunters and I did the Equitation finals on him. That was the horse that gave me my first taste of real success and made me realize that this was something that I wanted to do.

I rode Spanky for two and a half years as a junior, and I think I won the Massachusetts Medal Finals on him. I did my first time showing at Devon and Harrisburg and Washington with him. I may not have won all the classes, but at that point in my life, it was just a huge thrill to get to show at Devon. I think I was fifth in the Small Junior Stakes class there. That was a big moment for me.

I was not one of those extremely famous junior riders that was catch-riding a dozen hunters or anything like that. I had my one horse that wasn't even really mine that I got to ride, and I worked at my parent's farm and groomed. That's the best way to do it; come up the ranks and make yourself a better horseman.

After my junior years ended, I went to Boston College for four years, and I rode sort of sporadically during school. I mostly just rode in the summer. I started as a professional in the summers when I was at college but working for and under my dad at horse shows in the summertime. Basically, I was the low hunter queen. My dad rode all the younger horses or the higher-level hunters. But we had a group of amateur ladies and children, and I would school those horses during the week in the smaller hunter classes, so it was a great way to start because it wasn't super high pressure. It wasn't like I was riding and showing young horses that were purchased for me to bring along or to even be sold. I was just schooling them and hoping that they would be ready for their amateurs and juniors on the weekends.

After that, my first big hunter was a horse named Unseen. His barn name was Alex and I found him myself. We purchased him for a client, but I saw him and liked him and thought that I could develop and make him into a famous hunter. I showed him in the Pre-Green Hunters, then the First Year Greens and Second Year Greens. He was champion at Devon in 2001 with me in the Second Year Greens.

Not that long after being champion at Devon that year, I got my first client of my own, and her name is Megan McGuire. She's still a client and a friend. Megan sent me two horses, one was named Candlelight, and the other one was named Notre Dame. She sent them to my father's farm in Massachusetts, but they were very distinctly my clients. I went on to have a lot of success with them.

My advice for young riders is to not be in a rush to go out on your own, but spend a lot of time working for other people or working under people. Work for as many people as you can. Groom, ride, sit at the ring, and listen to people. I think that's all helpful. And secondly, I think it was important for me to take those four years to go to school. I think there's a lot of people in the industry that stop as juniors and then want to jump right into having a career as a professional, but those four years were really valuable for me and I think kids worry that people are going to forget about them or something if they take that time to go to school, but I don't believe that's true at all. I have a psychology degree and a minor in business, and the tools that I learned there, as well as the relationships I made, have helped me to get to where I am in my business.

Get Interactive
Click / Scan the QR Code Below

DON STEWART

Photo Courtesy Ramsey

ON STEWART, A PROMINENT FIGURE IN THE EQUESTRI-an world, has left an enduring mark on the sport through his decades-long journey as a top hunter rider and trainer. Renowned for his namesake stables and sales barn, Don Stewart Stables, his accomplishments in the equestrian arena are nothing short of extraordinary, earning him a plethora of distinguished honors and accolades.

Throughout his illustrious career, Stewart has secured multiple championship wins as both a rider and a coach at prestigious horse shows, including the Washington International, Devon, the Pennsylvania National, and the National Horse Show. His skill and expertise have consistently shone through in the show ring, making him a formidable force to be reckoned with.

Beyond his prowess as a rider, Stewart has also contributed significantly to the equestrian community. As chairman of the U.S. Hunter Jumper Association Junior Hunter Task Force, he has spearheaded important rule changes, most notably the introduction of a mandatory handy hunter class. His dedication to enhancing the sport's standards and fairness is a testament to his commitment to the welfare of both riders and horses.

Among his many victories, Stewart can proudly claim the 1969 Virginia Hunter-Seat Equitation Championship, multiple American Horse Shows Association Horse of the Year titles in the 1980s and 1990s, the 1989 Grand Champion Green Hunter Title at Harrisburg aboard Meant To Be, and the 1989 World Cup Working Hunter Classic riding Moment to Moment. In addition, he was awarded the Leading Hunter Rider title at the Devon Horse Show in 1992 and at the National Horse Show in 1993 and 1995.

Though Stewart sold his renowned business, Don Stewart Stables, in Ocala, Florida, he remains a pillar of the equestrian community nationwide. Alongside his wife, Nancy, they continue their equestrian journey by renting a farm in Ocala. The couple takes great pride in their three children, Don III, Whitney, and Erin. Erin has followed in her father's footsteps, evolving from a talented young rider who won top shows around the country as she progressed from ponies to junior ranks, to an accomplished professional equestrian. Under her father's guidance, Erin achieved a remarkable victory at the coveted ASPCA Maclay in 2002 and went on to claim the Grand Champion and Leading Rider titles at Capital Challenge and the Washington International Horse Show in 2009.

As both a rider and mentor, Stewart has exemplified dedication, skill, and passion, leaving a legacy that continues to inspire generations of equestrians to come.

❦ Lollipop Sparkle ❦

I'LL TAKE YOU ON A JOURNEY BACK TO WHERE IT ALL BEGAN, in Raleigh, North Carolina, at a place called The Pony Club. It was a quaint local spot, just about a mile away from my house, and it captured the hearts of everyone in our school. I still remember biking down there with my friends once a week for our riding lessons. If you're curious, you can find some nostalgic videos on YouTube under "Ruth Bason's Pony Club."

The Pony Club was more than just a riding school; it was a haven of fun and adventure. We'd all pile into a Volkswagen bus and head down there, ready for our riding lessons and eager to explore. During the week, we'd gallop through the woods, go on thrilling paper chases, and even embark on overnight rides. The place was brimming with activities like basketball, volleyball, and a swinging vine that let you soar above the river. It was a dream come true for any horse-loving kid like me, and I quickly fell in love with riding.

My first pony at The Pony Club was called Lollipop Sparkle, a steady and gentle companion. I guess they chose her for me because she barely had a pulse, which made her the perfect starting point. From there, I rode whoever they assigned me – Sparkle, Candy Cane, Sugarfoot, you name it.

At the age of 12, I got my first pony of my own, a sturdy 14.3 hand beauty named Can Do. He was a talented jumper, and together, we entered and conquered pony high jump contests, even clearing a fence as high as five feet three inches. It still stands as the highest jump I've ever accomplished to this day.

As I continued to grow and gain experience, my horse companions evolved as well. In the 1960s, I had the pleasure of riding a fine horse named Monday Blues. We competed in Junior Hunters and Equitation, as was the norm back then, before moving on to the Amateur Hunter classes. My journey then led me to Jimmy Lee in Virginia, where I honed my skills for a couple of years before joining Vicki Hansen's team in Wilmington, North Carolina. We were regulars on the Virginia Circuit during our younger days.

Things started to take a more serious turn in 1972 when a customer of mine placed fifth in the prestigious Maclay Finals. That success opened doors and set the stage for more achievements. In 1974, we made an impressive showing, securing third and fourth places in the Medal and Maclay Finals.

I eventually found myself predominantly focusing on the hunter division with Mary Reynolds, a character loved by all who knew her. In 1980, my hard work and dedication paid off when I garnered my first Horse of the Year award. This victory marked the beginning of an incredible run, earning Horses of the Year accolades for the next 12 years across various divisions.

Looking back, it's truly remarkable to see how far I've come from those humble beginnings at The Pony Club. It all started with one little pony, igniting a passion that has shaped my life and career. The equestrian world has been my home, and each step of the journey has been a cherished memory. I'm forever grateful for the wonderful horses and people who have been part of this incredible ride.

Get Interactive
https://www.instagram.com/donstewartstables
https://www.facebook.com/people/Don-Stewart-Stables
Click / Scan the QR Code Below

SCOTT STEWART

Photo Courtesy Sportfot

SCOTT STEWART, A LUMINARY IN THE EQUESTRIAN HUNTER world, is riding on a career studded with remarkable achievements. His name is synonymous with Grand Hunter Championships at prestigious events like Devon, Capital Challenge, and Indoors. His consistent excellence has also shone through in the fiercely competitive USHJA National Hunter Derby Series, where he has secured multiple triumphs.

One of the defining moments in Stewart's journey came in 2015 when he soared to victory as the USHJA International Hunter Derby Finals Champion, a testament to his exceptional skills and dedication to the sport. His reign of dominance extended to the Washington International Horse Show (WCHR), where he notched an incredible seven consecutive wins from 2007 to 2014, solidifying his reputation as a force to be reckoned with in the hunter world.

Stewart's illustrious career is a testament to his unwavering passion and commitment to the equestrian realm. Despite all the accolades and accomplishments, Scott Stewart remains grounded, always cherishing the memory of the first pony that set him on his equestrian journey.

❧ TROUBLE ❧

I GOT MY FIRST PONY WHEN I WAS 11 YEARS OLD. I HADN'T had any riding lessons, but my dad and I just went to the local dealer and bought a Saddlebred Palomino. She was about 14.2 and her name was Trouble. Sometimes she was trouble, but maybe it was more me than her, because I just didn't know the difference at that point!

She was a great pony. She did everything. I rode her Western and English. I did Pony Club, and the Mini Medal and Mini Maclays on her. I even drove Trouble with the sleigh in the wintertime and a carriage during the summer time. I kept her for about eight years. She lived on two acres in our backyard, in the suburbs of Connecticut, near Ox Ridge Hunt Club, where I eventually started working. My sister had another pony there also, and Trouble went everywhere with us. She went up and down the streets with us all day long. She did everything.

After I outgrew Trouble, I didn't really start showing seriously until I was probably 16 or 17 and began showing in the Equitation classes. I became a working student at a local barn called Silvermine Farm in Wilton, CT. I would ride whatever horses I could.

I then became a working student for Bill Ellis and I rode whatever he would let me ride. I rode with him until I had aged out of my Junior years. I showed in the Equitation mostly with him. I showed a few hunters, but at the time I wasn't very good at it. I did pretty well in equitation. I won the warmup at the Medal Finals and was called back for the second round of that Final in 1981. I was called back in the top ten at the Maclay Finals in 1982 and then I had a not-so-great afternoon round but it was successful in my mind.

After that, I started working for Ox Ridge Hunt Club, which was three miles from my house. I was 19 and I was in charge of showing the kids horses to get them ready. It was mostly an equitation barn at that point. I did work with Todd Karn and he had a couple of hunters that he qualified for Indoors. He left shortly afterwards, so I got to ride those horses at Indoors that year. That was really my first professional experience. I did the Regular Working Hunters, and I did okay. George Morris helped me there. He was training me while I was working at Ox Ridge. I ended up getting some good ribbons at The National Horse Show in New York that year. It may have been a little bit of a rough start, but I think I did okay.

It was a bit of a slow start, believe it or not, until I started seeing success. I had a horse called Gratis that was a beautiful black Warmblood that one of my customers bought and I started doing that in the First Year Greens and he had some success. He ended up getting sold to Charlie Weaver for Kelly Klein. Then I had a horse from Mimi Tashjian called Resaluution, who was Horse of the Year in the Green Confirmation Hunter division. I've been lucky and I've had a lot of really top horses since then who have won quite a few Horse of the Year honors in their divisions.

But at that point in my career, I was mostly training students and then eventually I moved to Old Salem Farm after being at Ox Ridge for 12 years. That's when I started doing the Hunters more. I won my first Champion at The National Horse Show during this time, riding Georgina Bloomberg's horse, Dialog L, so that was pretty special.

After that I went to New Jersey to work with Ken Berkley for River's Edge Farm, which I'm doing now. We've had a lot of nice and successful horses, especially with Betsee Parker, including Lucador and A Million Reasons. In 2021 I received a score of 100 riding Catch Me, an incredible horse that Becky Gochman owns. He had gotten a couple of scores of 97 and 98 over the prior few years, but when he got his 100, it was a perfect course for him. When I landed from the last fence I had a feeling it might happen, and I don't get that feeling very often.

Ken Berkley and I have been working together for almost 30 years. We have actually bred a few horses over the years, but mostly purchase 2 and 3 year olds in Europe and leave them at their farms overseas to grow up and get training. If we think they're good enough, we will bring them over to our farm when they are 4 or 5 years old. We probably have about 20 horses in Europe right now.

The advice I offer for young people starting out in the business who want to be successful is to find someone that you believe in that will take you under the wing and teach you the ropes a little bit. When I was younger, I pretty much rode whatever I could ride. It was just to get in the ring and get experience. My advice is to ride as many different kinds of horse as you can. Also, try to go to the horse show sometimes and just watch the professionals and see what they do.

Get Interactive
Click / Scan the QR Code Below

HUNT TOSH

Photo Courtesy Kind Media

HUNT TOSH, AN EXTRAORDINARY HUNTER RIDER, consistently pilots countless champions into the winners circle. However, each equine partner holds a special place in his heart. The years 2021 and 2022 saw Tosh triumphing in the USHJA International Hunter Derby Championship, capturing the prestigious title aboard Cannon Creek, the remarkable 2011 Holsteiner gelding owned by the esteemed Wheeler family. Tosh's success with Cannon Creek extended to the 2021 Pennsylvania National Horse Show, where they claimed the Grand Hunter Championship. His exceptional performances throughout the year also earned him the well-deserved title of 2021 Leading Hunter Rider.

Tosh's journey as a business owner began in his late teens when he ventured into buying and selling horses. Approximately 15 years ago, he forged a partnership with Betsee Parker and the Wheeler family, dedicating his expertise to developing, riding, and showcasing the horses they owned. Alongside his remarkable achievements with Cannon Creek, Tosh competes on another talented mount owned by the Wheelers, known as Autograph. Their combined efforts led them to victory at the prestigious Devon Horse Show in both 2022 and 2023. The duo has secured numerous tricolor ribbons at esteemed events along the east coast, including the Upperville Colt & Horse Show and the Pennsylvania National Horse Show.

Tosh's exceptional talent and dedication have not gone unnoticed in the equestrian world. He recently claimed the Emerson Burr Trophy, a testament to his remarkable horsemanship. Furthermore, in recognition of his outstanding achievements, Tosh was honored as the National Equestrian of the Year for 2022. His lifelong commitment to competitive horsemanship has been nothing short of extraordinary, and it all began with one pony—a testament to the humble beginnings that have paved the way for his remarkable success.

∽☙ Marvin ☙∾

I WAS LUCKY ENOUGH TO GROW UP ON A FARM. MY MOM WAS into steeplechasing, so we always had horses and ponies around. My older sister showed hunters and I had a white pony named Marvin who was a great pony. I probably fell off more than I stayed on though. I wasn't really into horse showing at an early age. I was more into trail riding, or trying to be a cowboy. But she was a great pony. I could take her in the woods, tie her to a tree, and hang out with her. She was like my best friend.

Marvin was my sister Martha's pony before mine. My grandfather bought her in Virginia, and then she was kind of a hand-me-down to me, but she was great. She was not only the pony I had that could go out in the woods and trail ride and bomb around on, but then they forced me at one point to finally take her to a horse show! That's where I think I made a true spectacle of myself, screaming and crying, because I was scared to death. But once they did that, I was hooked and here we are now.

My next horse was a horse named Teddy, who was a horse we had on the farm. The owner of the farm used him for driving. But I decided that I would ride him and teach him to jump. He was one I would take out and do the same thing, as with Marvin - trail ride, jump logs, jump all the stuff in the woods, do everything I could. I don't know if it was really done properly, but he was fun for a little boy to go out and play and mess around on.

After I had been jumping those two and messing around, then I moved on and started riding different ponies. My mom always had sale ponies and horses. I never had a pony that was necessarily my own, but there were lots of different ones that came and went, and I rode whatever I could get my hands on.

Then when I moved into the hunter ring with the junior horses, I did lots of catch riding on different horses and ponies for different trainers. I showed locally around Atlanta for years. I did a lot of local horse shows. I had an opportunity to go work for Roger and Judy Young when I was about 14. I started showing for them and did that for a few years. Then I was lucky enough to have Dennis Mitchell and Dennis Murphy take me under their wing and I started doing some jumpers and traveling around with them. I was doing a lot of catch riding at the horse shows for different people. Jack Towell was also one that helped me out. While his daughter Liza was in college, I was able to show some horses for them for several years. I just started doing lots of catch riding and I was able to ride whatever I could get on.

My first success with a hunter that I won on was a horse named Storm of Angels for Nancy Crosswell. We showed him for several years and then Nancy retired him in Atlanta at her farm and he lived out the rest of his life with her.

Now the tradition continues with my daughter Maddie. She is 17 this year. She's been champion quite a few times since she had a great pony career. She's now moved on to horses and she's had quite a lot of success.

What I tell her and what I tell all young equestrians is that this is a great lifestyle. I've been lucky enough to grow up in it and raise a child in it. My whole family is involved including my wife, Mandy. It's a great business that we're lucky to have. We get to spend time with our family every day while we're doing it. And the people that are in this industry all look out for each other. It's a great business because everyone truly looks out for each other. It accepts anybody. If you work hard enough and set your goals high enough, you can accomplish whatever you want. It truly accepted me for being a kid that was just getting going and people accepted me and gave me opportunities to get to where I am now. So, if you're willing to work at it and put in the hours and do your due diligence, you can get to whatever level you desire.

Get Interactive
Click / Scan the QR Code Below

LIZA TOWELL BOYD

Photo Courtesy Shawn McMillen

LIZA TOWELL BOYD IS AN ACCOMPLISHED RIDER AND trainer, hailing from Camden, South Carolina. Daughter of esteemed trainer, Jack Towell, they run Finally Farm Inc., which is known for training winning hunter riders under their guidance.

Towell Boyd's expertise lies in the show hunter world, and she has achieved great success in the sport. She has emerged as one of the country's top equestrian riders and trainers, consistently proving her skills and dedication. A highlight of her career was her impressive performance in the USHJA International and National Hunter Derbies. She has won over 25 championships in these events, showcasing her exceptional talent and expertise.

Her partnership with her beloved horse, Brunello, has been particularly remarkable. Together, they achieved victory in the prestigious USHJA International Hunter Derby Championships for three consecutive years, in 2013, 2014, and 2015.

Towell Boyd's achievements extend beyond hunter derbies. In the USHJA World Championship Hunter Rider program, she has established a record that remains unmatched. She is the only rider to have triumphed in the WCHR Pony, Junior, and Professional titles. She demonstrated her skill and versatility by securing these titles, highlighting her exceptional performance across different categories. Notably, Towell Boyd has also won the WCHR Professional Finals in both 2017 and 2018, further solidifying her reputation as a top-notch equestrian rider.

Even during her junior years, she showcased immense talent and promise. She was a three-time winner of the Overall World Champion Hunter Rider as a junior rider. Additionally, she placed second in the prestigious Washington International Equitation Finals and earned the Best Child Rider Award at the Washington International Horse Show an impressive four times.

Following her junior career, Towell Boyd pursued higher education and graduated from the College of Charleston in South Carolina. However, her passion for the horses led her back to the family business. Her influence extends to her own family as well. She is married to Blake Boyd, and together they have two daughters, Elle, and Adeline. The young girls are already following in their mother's footsteps and have begun their journey as aspiring equestrians.

Outside of Liza's accomplishments, her husband shares her passion for horses and has been involved in the equestrian world his entire life. Blake works as a licensed agent with EMO Agency, Inc., which is recognized as one of the country's top equine and farm insurance companies.

Overall, Towell Boyd's journey in the equestrian world is one of unparalleled success. Her dedication, talent, and achievements have solidified her position as one of the country's top riders and trainers, leaving an indelible mark on the sport.

❧ CASH AND CARRY ❧

Photo Courtesy Pennington

MY JOURNEY IN THE EQUESTRIAN WORLD BEGAN with a special pony named Cash and Carry. As a little black pony, he captured my heart and later became a beloved companion for my brothers Ned and Hardin. But even before Cash and Carry, there was another cherished pony in my life named Shamrock. I don't recall exactly how long I had him, but I've seen photos of me on his back as a tiny baby. In fact, my parents often remind me that I was introduced to ponies from the very day I came home from the hospital.

Cash and Carry, my Short Stirrup pony, holds a special place in my heart. He was an incredible teacher and a versatile pony. We shared countless bonding moments, from grooming and bareback riding to every aspect of horsemanship. He was truly an all-around great pony.

While ponies can sometimes be mischievous, none of them ever frightened me or made me want to shy away from the sport. Cash and Carry stayed with me for about two or three years before I moved on to another pony called Himself the Elf. He was truly remarkable and brought joy to numerous children who rode him. Together, we conquered Devon and the fall Indoors competitions.

Due to our family's sales barn and my father being a professional in the field, we had a constant flow of ponies coming and going. At a young age, I learned to love each pony dearly but also understood that they would soon find new homes with other young riders.

I vividly remember one particular pony being sold just before the Washington International Horse Show, and it was a saddening moment. However, my parents always ensured that there was another pony waiting in the wings. Even if one left, there was always another one occupying the stall next to it the very next day.

The first pony that truly marked a turning point in my career was For Kid's Sake. I started winning at Devon with her, and she became my pony of the year. We bought her as a four-year-old, and at the time, she came with a hefty price tag of $25,000, which was considered significant. It's interesting to reflect on this memory, as I recently watched an old VCR tape on Christmas night with my brother Hardin and my two children. Among the recordings was a video featuring For Kid's Sake. My mom shared the story of how we initially couldn't afford her, but on the way home, my parents decided they couldn't let her slip away and made a phone call from a payphone to secure the purchase.

Although we only had For Kid's Sake for a short period, she quickly became a top pony. Eventually, she was sold, likely to Don Stewart for one of his clients. However, as always, another pony was on the horizon. Tickled Pink entered my life, and together, we were the Large Pony and Grand Pony Hunter Champions at Pony Finals, held in Asheville that year before the event moved to Kentucky.

Green with Envy holds the distinction of being my first top horse. We tackled the Junior Hunters together, and he was quite exquisite. I believe he had some Thoroughbred blood. He played a significant role in teaching me to jump the 3'6" fences, as back then, there were no intermediate divisions between ponies and horses. The equestrian landscape has certainly changed since then, becoming much more technical and competitive. As an example, my eight-year-old daughter now competes in handy hunter classes with challenging trot jumps and rollbacks. The small pony division now tackles the same course as the 18-year-olds riding the large ponies, showcasing the increased complexity of the sport. While watching old videos of my performances at Harrisburg from years ago, I noticed that I had a pony who would swap leads in front of the jumps. My daughter remarked, "Oh, nowadays, that would have earned a 74 score." It's fascinating how the judging system has evolved over time.

Following Green with Envy, I had another incredible horse named Monday Morning. My mother, Lisa, has always possessed a keen eye for selecting horses, and Monday Morning was one of her exceptional choices. Even though he couldn't perform a lead change, he was an extraordinary horse who went on to win Horse of the Year. He remained my top horse until I aged out of the Junior division at 18. Once again, he was a Thoroughbred who imparted invaluable lessons to me.

During my time at the College of Charleston, I took a detour into the jumper ring. It was a delightful experience, and I would often meet my family at horse shows or venture to different competitions. My involvement felt more akin to being an owner, offering a different perspective and approach to the equestrian world.

Following college, I worked for an exceptional horsewoman named Sandy Labelle, who has since passed away. Her stable was in Virginia, and it provided me with a much-needed break from the family business. Working under Tom Wright further polished my skills, and it was a rewarding experience.

Eventually, I returned to the family business and became an integral part of it. It was during this time that my brother Hardin tried a horse named Brunello in Europe, intending to ride him once he arrived in the States. However, fate had different plans. When the horse completed quarantine, I was the first to ride him, and from that moment on, I never relinquished the reins. Brunello became my ultimate equine partner.

All these incredible experiences started with one little pony named Cash and Carry. He taught me so much and paved the way for the many ponies and horses that followed, leading me to the remarkable horse Brunello, who was honored as the 2015 Hunter Horse of the Year by The Chronicle of the Horse and the 2015 USEF National Horse of the Year. The memories and lessons from each of these equine partners have shaped my journey and instilled in me a deep love and appreciation for the equestrian world.

Get Interactive
http://www.finallyfarm.com/lizatowellboyd
Click / Scan the QR Code Below

JACK TOWELL

J ACK TOWELL HAS RIGHTFULLY EARNED HIS REPUTATION AS one of the nation's most accomplished trainers and developers of young riding talent. His journey as a hunter/ jumper trainer commenced at the tender age of 17, and since then, he has amassed an impressive list of achievements. With his guidance, over 75 champions and reserve champions have emerged at renowned events such as the Devon Horse Show in Pennsylvania, the Capital Challenge in Maryland, and the East Coast fall Indoor Finals, including the prestigious Pennsylvania National, Washington International, and National Horse Shows.

Jack's unparalleled expertise has garnered him numerous accolades. He stands alone as the only trainer to have been honored as the Pennsylvania National Horse Show Leading Junior Hunter Trainer a remarkable four times. Additionally, he holds the noteworthy distinction of being a four-time trainer of the overall World Champion Junior Hunter Rider. His students have earned the coveted Best Child Rider Honors on an astounding 14 occasions at both Devon and Indoors. They have also secured the title of Overall High-Score Pony Hunter at Pony Finals twice, as well as clinching the Championship title at Junior Hunter Finals.

Among his many achievements, Jack holds the distinction of training a Champion or Reserve Champion in every division at the prestigious year-end fall Indoor shows - an accomplishment that sets him apart as one of the nation's most versatile trainers.

In addition to his expertise as a hunter trainer, Jack has made significant strides in the jumper arena. His horses and riders have notched numerous victories in Grand Prix competitions. Furthermore, Jack's students have consistently showcased their skills in the equitation ring, securing top ribbons at all major Finals and even claiming victory at the esteemed Washington International Equitation Finals in 2006. To further underscore his contributions, Jack Towell was inducted into the National Show Hunter Hall of Fame as part of the esteemed Class of 2016.

In 2022, Jack Towell received the prestigious WCHR Old Spring-house Lifetime Achievement Award, a testament to his enduring impact and contributions to the equestrian community, presented during the Capital Challenge Horse Show. It is remarkable to think that this impressive journey all began with one little pony, a testament to the profound influence and transformative power of the equestrian world.

❧ CINDERS ☙

M Y JOURNEY WITH HORSES BEGAN WITH A LITTLE black Shetland pony named Cinders. He was a humble purchase at just $50, complete with a vibrant red Western saddle, breastplate, and bridle. Together, we explored the vast expanse of my grandfather's property in Morrisville, North Carolina, where I had a small one-acre area to call my own. Our adventures together were filled with laughter and excitement.

One memory stands out in particular - I would often climb up into my grandfather's fruit trees, indulging in juicy apples. When I spotted Cinders waiting below, I would leap from the limb straight into the saddle, embarking on spirited gallops. However, one unfortunate occasion saw me landing awkwardly on the saddle horn, an experience I would rather not repeat.

With a longing to emulate the thrilling jumps I witnessed at the Olympics, I realized that Cinders didn't possess the knowledge of how to jump. Undeterred, I devised a plan to teach him this new skill. I constructed a boarded-up stall, gradually increasing the height while enticing Cinders with the promise of grain.

To my delight, he embraced the challenge, eagerly leaping over each obstacle I presented. Soon, we were navigating a makeshift course of lounge chairs, bricks, and anything else I could gather. Cinders proved to be a remarkable partner in my quest for equestrian exploration.

As time passed, Cinders grew older, and eventually, he peacefully passed away. However, my father recognized the significance of our bond and purchased another pony for me at the sale. This time, a strawberry roan arrived, lacking much weight, and named Preacher Red due to his lean appearance. Like Cinders, Preacher Red also lacked knowledge in jumping. Thankfully, my father, a dedicated schoolteacher, sought guidance from Gordon Wright's book, "Learning How to Ride, Hunt, and Jump."

Together, we embarked on a journey of learning and growth. Settling in a picturesque hillside location, we set up jumps made of sticks and small trees. As I circled around, my father diligently read aloud from the instructional book, guiding me in honing my skills. He remained my steadfast support until my 16th birthday when he entrusted me with the keys to a truck, a small trailer, and a barn, empowering me to take charge of my equestrian pursuits.

That same year, I welcomed Bonnie Blue into my life, an exceptional little spotted mare standing at approximately 14.3 to 15 hands. Bonnie Blue possessed an incredible ability to jump vertical obstacles, though her width and obstacle skills were more limited. She had an uncanny knack for escaping fields and jumping out of five-strand barbed wire fences - a testament to her determination and spirit. Under our partnership, Bonnie Blue emerged as a formidable local Junior Jumper, defying the fences that sought to confine her.

There have been many horses since Cinders, Preacher Red, and Bonnie Blue. Each has contributed to my lifelong love affair with horses. Now, as a seasoned horseman, I am blessed to witness the next generation embracing this passion. My daughter, Liza Towell Boyd, achieved remarkable success at a young age, conquering ponies, and horses alike. She secured victories at the pony finals and emerged as the best junior rider, a title she held for multiple years. Following her footsteps, my son Hardin became a force to be reckoned with, triumphing at the Washington Equitation finals, and showcasing his talent at prestigious competitions such as Washington and Harrisburg. Their accomplishments have not only brought joy but also added immeasurable pride to my heart.

In 1982, my wife Lisa and I embarked on an exciting new chapter, establishing Finally Farm in Charlotte, North Carolina. Eventually, in 1989, we relocated the farm to its present location in Camden, South Carolina. Over the years, our riders and horses have clinched numerous Horse of the Year titles, Grand Prix victories, and Hunter Championships, cementing Finally Farm as one of the premier hunter/jumper stables in the Southeast.

What makes our journey more special is that Finally Farm remains a cherished family-owned and operated business. Alongside my daughter Liza Towell Boyd, who serves as a head trainer, we guide and nurture our students towards their equestrian dreams. Additionally, my son Hardin Towell manages his own business based in Wellington, Florida, but consistently lends his expertise during major competitions. Another family member, my son Ned, successfully runs Image Printing and Smitty's Printing in Camden.

Truly, this business reflects our shared commitment and passion. The horses have been our constant companions, propelling us forward in the pursuit of excellence. It all began with a little pony named Cinders, igniting a lifelong dedication to the equestrian world - an extraordinary journey that continues to shape and inspire us.

Get Interactive
http://www.finallyfarm.com/jacktowell
Click / Scan the QR Code Below

SAVANNAH UNGER

SAVANNAH UNGER IS A PASSIONATE SHOW JUMPING RIDER who thrives in the equestrian world, where her family plays an integral role in her journey. With her mother, Monique Kent, as her trusted trainer, her grandfather, Donald Kent, as a devoted supporter attending all her shows, and even her brother, Austin, offering assistance, the equestrian life has truly become a cherished family affair for Unger.

Hailing from Ocala, Florida, Unger and her family own and operate the esteemed Savannah Show Stables, LLC. Their shared commitment to horsemanship and the pursuit of excellence is evident in their collective efforts. Together, they travel as a unit, showcasing their talents and dedication on the competitive show jumping circuit.

Unger attributes her remarkable success to the unwavering support and guidance she receives from her family. Their collective expertise and encouragement have propelled her to new heights in the sport. Her recent victories, including an impressive two-time triumph in the $25,000 SmartPak Grand Prix at HITS Ocala, serve as a testament to her exceptional talent and unwavering determination.

As a show jumping rider, Unger embodies the spirit of resilience, precision, and elegance. Her innate connection with her equine partners enables her to navigate challenging courses with grace and skill. With each jump, she demonstrates an unwavering commitment to the sport she loves, always striving for perfection and continuously pushing the boundaries of her own capabilities.

Unger's passion for show jumping extends beyond the competition arena. She is deeply committed to the welfare and well-being of her horses, ensuring they receive the highest level of care and attention. This dedication translates into a harmonious partnership between horse and rider, characterized by mutual trust and respect.

Beyond her accomplishments as a rider, Unger is known for her kind and approachable demeanor. She exudes warmth and humility, always eager to connect with fellow equestrians, fans, and supporters. Her infectious enthusiasm for the sport and genuine love for horses inspires others, creating a ripple effect that fosters a sense of camaraderie within the equestrian community.

As Unger continues to make her mark in the world of show jumping, she remains grounded in her family values and the strong foundation they have provided. With her unwavering determination, undeniable talent, and the ongoing support of her loved ones, Unger is poised for a future filled with even greater achievements and continued success in the exhilarating world of show jumping.

MY EQUESTRIAN JOURNEY BEGAN WITH A SPECIAL pony named Ribbons. When I turned three, my mother gifted her to me. Ribbons had a reputation as a mischievous "lesson pony" known for throwing off kids, but she never bucked me off. We developed a unique bond, growing up together and exploring the world of riding. Though I didn't ask Ribbons to do the big jumps she was previously trained for, we had countless adventures and unforgettable moments.

Ribbons, a 12.1-hand Welsh cross pony, may not have been the fanciest pony, but she was versatile and eager to please. We dabbled in various disciplines, participating in hunter and jumper classes at local shows. We even ventured beyond the show ring - I once rode her down the road to the gas station and yes, even into the house! This was much to my mother's surprise, as she found this out when she discovered a photo on Facebook.

As I continued my equestrian journey, I transitioned to a Chincoteague pony named Teaga, who was a special Christmas gift.

Teaga took me to my first major show at the Kentucky Horse Park, where I found myself in a surprising encounter with an older competitor who told me that I was at the wrong ring with my pony. I assured her I was at the right ring, and my pony was competing against all the horses in her class. Despite the skepticism, we won the class, proving that determination and belief in oneself can overcome any doubts.

Throughout my riding career, I had the opportunity to ride several different horses. One memorable ride was a one-eyed horse who introduced me to traveling around the A Circuit as a junior rider. He had his quirks, but we formed a strong partnership, winning my first-ever Grand Prix on him. Another significant horse was Nana Mia, with whom I tackled true Grand Prix competitions. While we never won a Grand Prix together, Nana Mia was a reliable and safe partner who elevated my riding skills.

Two horses truly shaped my journey into the upper levels of the sport were Fundament E and Fabio. Fundament E, a fiery and hot-headed horse, presented challenges but also immense talent. He proved to be an unbeatable speed horse, and we secured numerous class victories together. Fabio, on the other hand, exhibited exceptional scope and a willingness to go above and beyond. He became the horse I won my first Grand Prix on, and his versatility in tackling larger courses brought me tremendous confidence.

The relationship I have with my horses is akin to having best friends. They understand me, challenge me, and teach me valuable lessons both on and off the field. Riding requires a deep sense of teamwork, and I am grateful for the support of my entire family throughout my career. My mother, who has been my coach since day one, possesses a wealth of experience and has guided me with unwavering dedication. My grandfather's presence at all my shows provides a sense of comfort and encouragement. Even my brother and father, while not horse people themselves, have always shown their support in their unique ways.

I want to acknowledge the behind-the-scenes work that goes into being an equestrian. The paperwork, training, and preparation for shows often go unnoticed by those outside the equestrian world. I appreciate my family's commitment and the teamwork we share in managing Savannah Show Stables, LLC, which we own and operate in Ocala, Florida.

To aspiring riders, I offer words of encouragement. The equestrian industry may present obstacles, whether financial, familial, or otherwise, but perseverance is key. Hard work and determination can propel you from humble beginnings to remarkable achievements. Closed doors may surround you, but keep knocking, for eventually, one will open. Remember that bad days are inevitable, but the good days become all the more rewarding.

As I continue my journey as a young rider, I am fortunate to have grown up with horses like Fundament E and Fabio. We have shared the growth and triumphs together, building a bond that transcends words. I am also grateful for the unwavering support of my boyfriend, Patrick, who understands the equestrian lifestyle and stands by my side.

Get Interactive
https://www.facebook.com/Savannahshowstablesllc/
Click / Scan the QR Code Below

AARON VALE

AARON VALE IS UNDENIABLY ONE OF THE MOST ACCOMplished and revered Grand Prix riders in the United States, with a remarkable career filled with an array of achievements. Holding an impressive record of 275 wins and counting, Vale has set new benchmarks in the equestrian world. Notably, he holds records for the most Grand Prix wins in a single year and the highest amount of prize money won in a single year, showcasing his exceptional talent and consistency in the sport.

Vale's exceptional skills and achievements have led to him being selected to represent the United States Equestrian Team (USET) on European Tours and in Nations Cups. Additionally, he has achieved significant success in the World Cup Finals, demonstrating his ability to compete at the highest level of international show jumping.

Beyond his prowess in show jumping, Vale has showcased his versatility by excelling in other disciplines as well. As a junior rider, he has earned the prestigious title of Reserve Champion at all three of the Nation's Equitation finals, including the Maclay, Medal, and USET. His outstanding performances have also earned him the recognition of being named the Best Child Rider at renowned competitions such as the Washington International Horse Show and the Pennsylvania National Horse Show.

Vale's dominance extends into the realm of hunter competitions, where he has secured numerous victories in both the USHJA Hunter International and National Derbies. He has triumphed twice in the highly esteemed $500,000 Diamond Mills Hunter Prix, further solidifying his status as an exceptional talent in the hunter discipline.

Internationally, Vale has showcased his skills across the globe. He has also represented his country as part of the Nations Cup teams, showcasing his ability to perform under intense international pressure. Throughout his illustrious career, Vale has claimed victories in numerous distinguished competitions. Notable among his achievements are the Queen's Cup in Barcelona, Spain, and his three-time triumph in the Washington International President's Cup. He has also placed in the prestigious World Cup Finals.

Currently, Vale manages his own farm, Thinkslikeahorse, in Williston, Florida, where he continues to train and compete at the highest level of the sport. He shares his life and passion for horses with his wife, the accomplished equestrian Mallory Vale, and together, they are raising their talented daughter, Kinser, who is already immersed in the world of competitive equestrian events.

❦ MISS PICKLE ❧

I HAD A COUPLE OF FIRST PONIES. MY VERY FIRST PONY WAS Miss Pickle. She was a gray and white paint; a Leadline type of pony. My parents used to turn her out in the arena because that was the only extra turnout space they had. My parents weren't very smart because they used to tie the gate shut with a leather lead shank or something similar. The pony would chew through it, and she'd get out. So then they'd have to go around town looking for her. This didn't happen once; this was a regular occurrence that my pony was missing for a day or two.

My next first pony came along because my mom was working for Las Colinas in Texas. Originally, they were focused on Western, but when they started an English section, my mom became the trainer for that. They had a pony there that wasn't good enough for reining or whatever kind of western stuff they did.

The pony's name was La Sassy and he became my pony. He was quite a good jumper and had a really good set of knees. I was only eight years old, and I was fairly successful with him showing. We'd go to the hunter/jumper shows in Texas. By the time I got proficient enough to be really competitive, we were protested against on the pony's size, so they measured him. He was a little closer to 14.3 than 14.2, so we got kicked out of the pony division.

When I wasn't more than 10 or 11 years old, my mom sent me to the Fredericksburg Horse Show with Colonel Russell to look at a couple of horses. The horse show was at a fairground, way out in the middle of nowhere in the center field of a training race-track. Back then, you only had one class a day in each division. So I showed the horses for three days during a Friday, Saturday, and Sunday horse show. By Sunday, I got a third place in the Stakes class on one horse. The other horse was a nice old gray mare, really sweet and all, but she stopped that day, threw me off, and ran out of the arena! Then she jumped the inside rail of the racetrack, jumped the outside rail of the racetrack, then ran back to the stables.

My mom bought me a horse after the show. It was not the horse that I was third on in the Stakes class. She bought me the horse I fell off. So it was quite a fun journey. The mare's name was Storyteller and we bought her as a five-year-old. After I got Storyteller, a month or so later, we had a barn horse show. We had another refusal at a fence, and then the horse reared up after stopping at the fence. My mom ran the barn, so that was not exactly great advertising in front of the customers.

A few months later, at another horse show, we were showing on a grass field and just had those triangle flags as the perimeter of the arena. When I went to take my 5th place ribbon, my horse spooked. She was very scared of the ribbon and she started running. She ran right through the flag fencing of the arena! We were out in the country and that area had been bare cut a few years before. So now it was all scrub brush, with little trees that were eight or ten feet tall. Finally, she got deep enough into the brush that she couldn't keep running. So, that's what saved me.

About a year later I was state champion in the Junior Hunters in Texas with her. Back then, we only had Limit Hunters, and when you won six blues, you were into the Junior Hunters. I was champion at my first show when I got out of limits in the juniors.

Another time, I was showing in the Pre-Green Hunters against all the professional riders. There weren't nearly as many divisions as there are today, but this was a fairly important division. I won the first class and then the next day I won the class again. At the time I felt like I would gladly give both classes back if I could win the Stakes class because that class awarded a hundred dollars! That was big money back then, around 1978. Sure enough, I won the stakes. I won all three classes and was the Champion, against all the professionals there.

That was Storyteller. Other than Miss Pickle and La Sassy, I have to say that Storyteller was my first horse that I had notable accomplishments on. Although, I was still young enough that she could have been considered my first pony.

Now my nine-year-old daughter, Kinser, is a rider. She's about to start in the meters soon with her ponies. She wants to jump higher. She wants to go faster like her daddy. She wants to know what the prize is. She wants the prize.

All these equestrian experiences have come around because of my first pony.

Get Interactive
http://www.thinkslikeahorse.com
Click / Scan the QR Code Below

KRISTEN VANDERVEEN

Photo Courtesy Michelle Williams

KRISTEN VANDERVEEN IS A HIGHLY ACCOMPLISHED equestrian who runs Bull Run Jumpers, a prestigious training and sales stable located in the equestrian hub of Wellington, Florida. Remarkably, she took on the responsibility of managing the stables at the young age of 18, showcasing her exceptional talent and maturity beyond her years.

With her current equine partners, Kristen has experienced a string of remarkable successes. Together, they have formed an extraordinary bond that has propelled them to the forefront of the show jumping world.

In recognition of her exemplary sportsmanship and character, Vanderveen was awarded the Horse & Style Magazine Style of Riding Award in 2021. This prestigious accolade celebrates riders who demonstrate respect, dignity, and courtesy both in and out of the show ring. Vanderveen's unwavering commitment to these values has earned her the admiration and respect of her peers and equestrian enthusiasts alike.

Furthermore, Vanderveen's noteworthy performance during the Winter Equestrian Festival (WEF) in Wellington, Florida, led to her receiving the esteemed Martha Jolicoeur Leading Lady Rider Award in 2021. This award acknowledges Kristen's outstanding achievements and contributions as a female equestrian, recognizing her as a leading figure within the show jumping community.

Beyond her accomplishments in the arena, Vanderveen is instantly recognizable with her signature ponytail, which has become a distinctive part of her image. Known for her lightning-fast riding style, she captivates spectators with her thrilling and dynamic performances, consistently pushing the boundaries of speed and precision in the show jumping arena.

❦ WILDFLOWER ❦

Photo Courtesy Michelle Williams

M Y FIRST PONY WAS NAMED WILDFLOWER. I RE-
member I loved her, but every time I got to a
corner, she would just turn the corner and I'd
slip right off the side of her. And every single
time they'd throw me back up on her and she'd go through a
turn, and I would fall right off of her again. She was a cute, big
pony and was super sweet.

After Wildflower, I had a pony named Pinky, who was the op-
posite of Wildflower. Pinky went around with her ears pinned
back. She'd had plenty of kids who rode her in the past and
she had done the Pony Hunters, so she definitely taught me the
ropes. But she was kind of your typical pony; a little bit grouchy
and she had a little bit of a sour expression, but she was a good
girl. I think I only had her for a year or so and then I was done
with Pony Hunters. I got a pony jumper who was the coolest
Hackney pony I had ever seen. She used to pull carts and then I

got her and we started jumping her. Her name was Supersonic. I went to Pony Jumper Finals with her and that's kind of what got everything going for me, and I never did the hunter divisions again after that.

My first jumper was a horse named Heidi Ho. She was a Grand Prix horse already and I was lucky enough to have her. She did my very first jumpers after graduating from the ponies and she took me all the way to my first Grand Prix. She was a really cool horse. I think riding her is what gave me the love for going fast. She always wanted to get to the other side.

I had Heidi for a while, probably five years. When I moved on she went to another girl who was going to retire her.

After that, I had a horse named Blue Bayou. He was more the middle ground, a solid Junior Jumper. I only had him for a year and then I got Bradbury who was my first Grand Prix-type horse, but he was also just leased for a year. That horse was nuts! He would just run and nobody else wanted to ride him. He ended up with Laura Chapot - the only other person crazy enough to ride him. But he was great. I took him to Indoors and to the Junior Jumper Championships and Young Riders.

Charlie Brown was next. Charlie Brown was the first, all-on-my-own purchase as a young professional. Charlie taught me a lot. We did all the Grand Prix classes, and we even did the Budweiser Invitational. He was my first real Grand Prix horse that could go to all the events. I had Charlie for three years and then he got sold and went on to do some smaller jumper divisions. He then ended up doing the 3'6" Equitation in his older age and he still does it today. Honestly, he's very old now!

After Charlie, I got a horse that we called Eternal, who was my first real FEI horse. I thought he was a real Olympic prospect. At the time that was the best horse I had ever ridden. He won all kinds of Grand Prix classes. I went one year to Colorado and I think I won four out of the five or four out of the six Grand Prix classes all in a row for that circuit. I won my first FEI class with him in Wellington. He won everywhere we went. He was just a phenomenal horse. I had him for a long time and then my clients ended up buying him and I got to teach him doing one meter jumpers. So he ended up with a good, easy life at the end.

Now I have my own stables called Bull Run. I have changed my business model a little bit to where I also have clients and some sale horses. We have 23 horses inside the barn that I'm in charge of, but I would say for myself, I probably have four higher-level horses with another two to four that are kind of in the making behind them. I am looking forward to their success.

When it comes to looking ahead, my advice to young riders would be to stay patient and stay focused on your goals. Try not to get distracted by comparing yourself to other people. I think that is important. That and what also helped me too, is to really stay focused on what I'm doing and what my calling is in the sport, and not get distracted by comparing myself to other people.

Get Interactive
https://www.fei.org/athlete/10039572
Click / Scan the QR Code Below

110

MCLAIN WARD

MCLAIN WARD, AN ESTEEMED AMERICAN EQUESTRI-an, has made an indelible impact on the world of showjumping through his exceptional talent and unwavering dedication to the sport. Despite a challenging start with ponies, it was when Ward transitioned to horses that his skills truly flourished. His rise to prominence was nothing short of remarkable, earning him the nickname "The Kid" due to his early successes. At the age of 14, in 1990, he became the youngest rider to win the United States Equestrian Federation's Show Jumping Derby, followed by another record-breaking feat as the youngest rider to win the USET Medal Finals, both accomplished in the same year. With the unwavering support of his equestrian professional parents, Ward's passion for riding continued to grow, and he understood that every journey begins with a pony.

Ward's prowess as a rider skyrocketed, leading to a series of phenomenal achievements throughout his career. One notable highlight was his back-to-back victories at the esteemed Hampton Classic Grand Prix in 1998 and 1999, where he partnered with his Selle Francais bay gelding, Twist Du Valon, becoming the first rider-horse combination to accomplish such a feat. This remarkable achievement firmly established Ward as a force to be reckoned with in the world of show jumping.

His determination and commitment propelled him even further, making him the youngest rider ever to surpass the $1 million prize money mark in grand prix competition in 1999. This milestone set a new standard for aspiring equestrians worldwide, showcasing Ward's unwavering drive to excel.

In 2004, Ward achieved a lifelong dream as he represented the United States at the Olympic Games. He played a vital role in the team's victory in team jumping, earning a well-deserved gold medal. This triumph solidified his place among the elite riders in the world, and his dedication to the sport shone brightly.

Throughout his career, Ward continues to capture victories and the hearts of spectators worldwide, leaving an enduring legacy in the world of show jumping. He has been named to represent the United States in countless Nations Cup competitions, World Equestrian Games, World Cup Finals, and Olympic Games. With extraordinary partners such as Sapphire, Rothchild, HH Azur, Clinta, Contagious, and Callas, Ward has consistently set his name at the top of the Longines FEI World Rankings year after year.

PETER PAN ONE & PETER PAN TWO

Photo Courtesy Pennington

I STARTED WITH TWIN PONIES; PETER PAN ONE AND PETER PAN Two. They were little black ponies who had lived together their whole lives. One was blind. I don't know where my father found them, but they were safe and got me started.

The first pony I showed was called Dina Dan from Jack Trainer who had won at Devon and all over the country. By the time I got him, I think he was probably nearing about 30 and was just the right teacher. I can't say I had any big success with him or any pony. It was more like they took care of me. You see, I wasn't thought to be a very good rider at the time. It was well down the road when I started to get on the jumpers and the equitation, things started to go in a better direction for me, and the rest is history.

As a matter of fact, there's a funny story about Artie Hawkins and Linda Andrisani who were judging me at Fairfield one year.

Linda said to Artie, who was a friend of my dad's, "You've got to tell Barney not to push his kid because he doesn't have a lick of talent!"

But it all worked out.

The horse I am most proud of is a chestnut named Rothchild. It's an interesting story because he's a horse I didn't care for very much in the beginning. I didn't want to buy him. I didn't like his character, but I was advised to take the chance anyway, and we developed a relationship and went on to have a lot of success. It just goes to show that with a lot of perseverance and hard work, you can end in a good place.

Rothchild was the last horse my father picked out for me before he passed away from cancer in 2012. That was a nice horse that went on to do very well at the World Championships. And he was a big money winner and won over $3 million. So, we had a nice career. That was one of my favorite horses. He was a cool horse, and he was different. He wasn't necessarily the most talented horse in the whole world, but he had a good character, and he was a competitive horse. And you know that makes up for a lot.

My horse, Sapphire, came before him. And even before Sapphire, there was a horse called Orchestra. That was my first kind of top horse. He would stop a little bit, but he was good. And then Sapphire came along. We went to two Olympic Games, two gold medals, two World Championships. She really had an incredible career. Now I have HH Azur. I have been very lucky to have all these great horses.

Azur was found by a partner of ours in Europe. I tried her once and didn't buy her and went back a second time and ended up buying her that time. Sometimes you're meant to be with a certain horse.

We recently participated in the Family Class at Upperville and that was a funny story because a mutual friend of ours had recommended it and supplied the horses. And you know the Family

Class is more important than the Grand Prix at Upperville and I'm a Yankee. So, as we were getting our blue ribbon, I noticed that we needed to exit quickly, or we might not get out of there alive! I'm joking, but it was fun, and my daughter loved it. We enjoyed it a lot.

McLain Ward's equestrian journey, from his humble beginnings with ponies to the heights of global competition, serves as an inspiring testament to the power of perseverance, hard work, and the indelible bond between a rider and their equine partner. With a collection of exceptional horses and a legacy of accomplishments, Ward continues to captivate audiences and etch his name among the greatest in the sport.

Get Interactive
https://www.mclainward.com
Click / Scan the QR Code Below

SHARN WORDLEY

Photo Courtesy Andrew Ryback Photography

SHARN WORDLEY IS AN ACCOMPLISHED SHOW JUMPING RIDer from New Zealand who has made a name for himself in the international equestrian community. He has achieved numerous accolades and represented his country at prestigious events around the world.

Wordley's journey began with his participation in the Beijing Olympic Games in 2008, where he proudly represented New Zealand. His talent and dedication also earned him a spot at the FEI World Equestrian Games in 2018, where he continued to show his skills on a global stage.

Throughout his career, Wordley has competed in 22 countries. As a young rider, he was crowned the champion in New Zealand, highlighting his early success in the sport. Living in Europe, Wordley competed in renowned shows like CSIO5* Rome, CSIO5* Lummen, and CSIO 5* Hickstead, among others, solidifying his presence in the international show jumping circuit.

Beyond his achievements as a rider, Wordley has also ventured into coaching. He has guided riders who have represented their countries in prestigious events such as the Olympics, World Cup Finals, World Championships, and the Pan American Games. His expertise and mentorship have contributed to the success of his proteges.

Wordley is married to Lauren Balcomb, an Australian equestrian. Together, they form a supportive partnership as he continues to pursue excellence in the show jumping arena.

Furthermore, Wordley is a co-founder and partner of Wordley Martin Equestrian, a company specializing in premium equestrian surfaces, arena and gallop track design and installation, site preparation and construction, and custom footing and equestrian facility products. Founded in 2008 alongside Craig Martin, another international show jumping athlete, the company offers comprehensive solutions to create ideal riding environments for equestrians.

❦ JOSEPHINE ❦

WHEN I WAS A KID, I HAD RIDING LESSONS AT A LIT-tle, local riding school that used to take you down the beach. The riding coach sold my mum and me a four-year-old, freshly broken-in, chestnut mare, for $400. That mare tried to kill me every time I sat on her. Josephine was her name. She kept jumping out of the paddock and running down the freeway. Also, I fell off her every time I got on. So I don't think she had been finished being broken in, but we kept her for about eight months.

Then I moved on to a pony called Shawnee who was the oppo-site. He was half dead. He was probably in his 20s. I had him for about a year until he passed away. But he was a good pony. His favorite gate was standing still.

I had several ponies growing up because we jumped ponies until we are 16 years old in New Zealand. I was jumping Grand Prix ponies because we have a Grand Prix series in New Zealand for ponies, just like for horses.

My first main jumping horse was called Marco and he was a great horse. I bought him for USD $2500 at the time and I won the New Zealand young rider championships with him. He was also second in the Horse of the Year. I took him overseas, where he jumped the Masters at Spruce Meadows. Then I took him to Europe and he jumped Rome and St. Gallen and the Hickstead Derby. He jumped around all of the World Cup shows in Europe. He was a great guy. He made up for the first pony! I was an amateur with no experience and I was jumping the biggest shows in the world. He saved me all the time. He was my learning curve horse.

Marco retired with me and later died. Since then, I've ridden thousands of horses but he was the horse that made a big difference for my career.

Then I had a very good horse for Glenwood Springs. He jumped the smaller Grand Prix classes, but he was very competitive. Next, there was a horse called Mr. Flanagan who must have won at least 20 Grand Prix classes with me. He was an Irish horse that I bought and he was instrumental in my career. I had a horse called Derly Chin De Muze. Eric Lamars had that one. He took it to the London Olympic Games in 2012 and I got her after that. I was third in the American Invitational on that one. I placed in some really big shows with Derly Chin De Muze.

Believe it or not, the Olympics for me was a good and bad experience. The horse that I was planning on taking got injured and then my younger horse was doing quite well. He was not so reliable, but he was a good jumper. They ended up putting him on the team and he got to the Olympic Games and couldn't handle the atmosphere. He kind of shrunk when he got in the ring the first day, and I had nine rails down the first day at the Olympic Games. It was probably one of the hardest moments in my whole career to be in that situation. It was one of the hardest parts of my career, but there were a lot of positives in it too because now if I ever have a bad round, it's "not as bad as that, right?"

Since the age of 10, I dreamed about going to the Olympics, finally got there, knocked down nine rails on the first day. It was mortifying. But I moved on. You must! What doesn't kill you makes you stronger so no one can complain to me about having bad days. And I can't complain to myself about having bad days either.

Get Interactive
https://wordleymartin.com
Click / Scan the QR Code Below

A portion of the proceeds from the sale of this book will be donated to support Danny & Ron's Rescue, a non-profit dog rescue based in South Carolina. Danny and Ron rescue dogs into their home, embrace them as their own, and help them find forever homes.

www.DannyRonsRescue.org

ABOUT THE AUTHORS

DANNY PATE

DANNY PATE, HAILING FROM LANDRUM, SOUTH CAROLINA, is a renowned figure in the horse racing industry, particularly known for his expertise as a pinhooker and juvenile consignor. With a career spanning six decades, he has left an indelible mark on the world of horse trading and training.

Having grown up in Landrum, Pate's early equestrian experiences revolved around riding quarter horses. However, it was his partnership with esteemed horsemen George Webster, Bill Bremer, and Gerald Pack that would prove pivotal in shaping his future in the industry. Under their guidance, he began foxhunting, and his passion for horses grew exponentially.

During his formative years, from the age of 16 to 26, Pate rode Amateur steeplechase races, showcasing his natural talent and affinity for working with horses. In the early 1990s, he took on the role of managing Golden Orb Farm, a significant milestone in his career, as it was the place where the multiple graded stakes winner and millionaire Glitter Woman was foaled and raised.

In 1996, Danny made a bold move by purchasing a 70-acre farm in the Starting Point Complex, located north of Ocala, Florida. He further expanded his operation by leasing an additional 50 acres. The inspiration for the farm's name, Solitary Oak Farm & Training Center, came from a majestic oak tree that stood alone in the track infield. This acquisition marked a turning point in his career, as he established a training center focused on preparing horses for racing, honing his skills in the process.

It was during this phase that Pate found his true calling: training horses for races and excelling as a pinhooker and consignor at the 2-year-old sales. His keen eye for talent and deep understanding of equine potential allowed him to purchase, sell, and train numerous exceptional horses over the years, making him one of the country's leading pinhookers.

As a testament to his dedication and accomplishments, Pate has worked with numerous grade 1 stake horses, solidifying his reputation as an authority in the industry. His name has become synonymous with excellence and expertise in pinhooking and horse training.

Beyond his illustrious career in the horse racing world, Pate's passion has now shifted towards the realm of reading and writing. As a true lover of literature, he has embarked on a new venture, authoring the first book in an exciting series, showcasing his versatility and creativity beyond the equestrian world.

With a legacy spanning decades, Pate's journey from a young horse enthusiast in South Carolina to a leading figure in the racing industry is a testament to his unwavering commitment and passion for all things equine. His contributions have left an enduring impact on the sport and continue to inspire those who follow in his footsteps.

MICHAEL BEAS

MICHAEL ALEXANDER BEAS, A PROMINENT FIGURE in the realms of finance, publishing, marketing, and brand management, has traversed a remarkable professional journey. With over 12 years of invaluable experience in Fortune 500 companies, he eventually embraced entrepreneurship. Presently, Michael serves as the founder of Altas Elite Publishing, the founder and CEO of eBook Marketing Solutions, and the CEO of the esteemed dance music publication, Raver Magazine.

Recognized as an authority in book marketing, Michael possesses a remarkable talent for rebranding over 1,000 books, propelling them to the status of bestsellers. Additionally, he has authored and published an impressive collection of over 7,000 articles while personally conducting interviews with some of the most influential figures in the dance music industry. Michael's unwavering passion lies in revolutionizing his field and assisting authors and music producers in achieving the same feat.

Leveraging his extensive background in coding and search engine optimization (SEO), he enables his clients to navigate the digital landscape with unprecedented success.

Prior to establishing his own ventures, Michael honed his skills in revenue generation within esteemed organizations in the banking, telecommunications, and commercial business insurance sectors. Notable among them are Citibank Financial, Lucent Technology, AVAYA Communications, and Liberty Mutual.

Michael's academic prowess includes degrees in Business Administration, Business Management, and Marketing from Nova Southeastern University. In addition to his remarkable professional achievements, he is also an accomplished author with two books to his credit. With an insatiable appetite for knowledge, Michael remains dedicated to reading and publishing, with numerous forthcoming books eagerly anticipated and his passion to help restore dignity and self-worth in the prison rehabilitation system in America is quickly inspiring others to make a change for the better.

Instagram: @BeasMichael

www.atlaselitepublishingpartners.com

www.ingramcontent.com/pod-product-compliance
Lightning Source LLC
Jackson TN
JSHW011209060525
83799JS00007B/13